RAISE YOUR CHILD'S SOCIAL IQ

Stepping Stones to People Skills for Kids

Advantage Books

CATHI COHEN, L.C.S.W.

Advantage Books

Copyright © 2000 by Advantage Books

All rights are reserved. No part of this book may be reproduced by any process whatsoever without the written permission of the copyright owner.

Library of Congress Cataloging-in-Publication Data

Cathi Cohen, 1960-

Raise Your Child's Social IQ: Stepping stones to people skills for kids / Cathi Cohen.
p.   cm.

ISBN 0-9660366-8-9

1. Social skills in children handbooks, manuals, etc.

2. Child rearing handbooks, manuals, etc.

3. Parenting handbooks, manuals, etc.

I. Title.

HQ783.C59   2000   99-39733
                                                                          CIP

Cover Design by Karen Monaco
Cartoons by Joe Mirabello

Published by
Advantage Books
3268 Arcadia Place NW
Washington DC 20015

10   9   8
Printed in the U. S. A.

TABLE OF CONTENTS

▶ Introduction   v

▶ How To Use This Book   ix

▶ Getting Started   1

▶ Joining In   24

▶ Communicating and Conversing   41

▶ Reading Social Signals   64

▶ Raising Self-Esteem   84

▶ Coping with Teasing   116

▶ Managing Stress   148

▶ Solving Social Problems   166

▶ Resolving Conflicts   186

▶ Managing Anger   204

▶ Putting It All Together   225

▶ Afterword—For parents of Children with Special Needs   229

I'D LIKE TO THANK . . .

‣ the parents and children in the Stepping Stones groups. These families shared with us their personal stories and struggles. I admire them for their dedication to each other and to the healing process. Their experiences and ideas illuminate this book.

‣ the In Step staff (past and present), Barbara Caceres, Cecilia Berg Benson, Barbara Eckman, Keith Ewell, Rebecca Fleischer, Malinda Gray, Mitchell Harrow, Elisa Human, David Kerrigan, Jennifer Lager, Ron Leiberman, Judith McCrosky, Helen Power, Nancy Reder, James Sebben, Rho Silberglitt, Wes Smith, and Sharon Watson, whose tireless work, creative ideas, and professional expertise further developed the work of Stepping Stones. They each made numerous contributions to the process, and made the social skills training work fun and exciting.

‣ Peter Robbins, M.D., who had the sensitivity to see the need for Stepping Stones and the vision to encourage its development.

‣ Margaret King, my office administrator, dedicated cheerleader, idea woman, and resident mother, without whose clear understanding and forethought I would be lost (literally and figuratively) most days.

‣ Patricia Quinn and Kathleen Nadeau, my publishers at Advantage books, who have been forever patient and supportive in the seemingly never-ending process of writing this book, and who have helped me feel that I had something to share with parents and their children.

‣ Lori Heyman, my dear friend and editor of this book, who took on the job of this careful and time-consuming work without complaint. Both personally and professionally, she will pursue nothing short of excellence, and I feel grateful that she used these skills to help mold my writing into a book.

‣ and lastly, but most importantly, my children, Jesse, Dov, and Lyana, from whom I learn something new every day. Without their encouragement and willingness to give me the time to write, I would most certainly still be writing into the next century!

INTRODUCTION

An eight-year-old boy once said to me, "I feel like I live on my *own* planet, and everyone else lives on *this* one!" What he was describing was his feelings of loneliness and disconnection from other kids his age. This can be terribly distressing for a child. Think about it. Children are around other kids all day—in the classroom, during recess, on the schoolbus, and at extracurricular activities. For a child lacking in social skills, these occasions can be pressure-filled and isolating. Going to school becomes something to dread and friendships, if they exist, may offer more pain than solace.

Without the friendship of peers, children feel alone, confused, and out of sync with the rest of the world. And these feelings can have serious repercussions for their future. Research has found that children with poor peer relationships are more likely to later develop serious problems such as low academic performance, depression, failed relationships, poor parenting skills, and troubled careers. Friendship clearly plays a vital role in a child's emotional health and well-being.

A child with a high "social IQ" is one who has acquired the skills necessary to make and keep friends. This is a child who gets along easily with others, has high self-esteem, actively listens when spoken to, and resolves conflicts using nonviolent means. Instinctively understanding what is expected of him, the child with a high social IQ can effortlessly size up a social situation. This child easily can join a group of children playing and "go with the flow." The socially competent child doesn't have to learn these skills. They seem to come quite naturally.

When parents and peers behave in appropriate ways, the socially adept child automatically learns from them and internalizes the lessons. These children generally do not need any formal training in social skills. But not all children are so fortunate.

For children who struggle in social situations, there are very few opportunities available to learn social skills. Our schools don't commonly teach such subjects as cooperation, empathy, conflict resolution, managing emotions, and communication skills. Our society assumes that all children learn how to get along with others by just observing how others behave. Not true! For many children, being in socially challenging situations is the hardest part of their day. For these kids, solving a complex mathematics problem is easier than carrying on a conversation with a friend. For them, learning an advanced computer game is great fun, while listening and responding appropriately to a friend's problem is pure torture. A child can be a straight "A" student and still need to raise his social IQ. Children with these kinds of social skill issues have what I call "social learning disabilities."

The *good* news is that poor social skills can improve with coaching. You, as a parent, can learn techniques to help your child, and the positive results can be rapid and dramatic.

I've been counseling children, adolescents, and their families for 15 years. The majority of kids I see in therapy complain about feeling left out. They'd like to fit in better, but they have no idea how to do it. Social skills are hard to learn in individual and family therapy sessions. Children may appear warm, confident, and connected in the safety of their family or in a one-on-one counseling session. But they can behave very differently in a group at school, in the neighborhood, or at a social gathering.

Children learn social skills best in the company of other children. It's difficult to teach kids the skills they need to get along with others when they're alone with a therapist in the artificial atmosphere of the office. Even though we can role-play how to have a conversation or how to negotiate a conflict, the children continue to complain about problems with their peers. A child can tell me his perspective on a fight with a classmate at school, but he cannot enlighten me on the other child's perspective. He remembers the consequences of the argument, but not what led up to the altercation. I have continually felt frustrated trying to help children through individual counseling sessions because I couldn't witness their conflicts happening in real life.

Parents are usually very willing to help their children learn social skills, but they need guidance. Parents want to help their children make the friends they so strongly desire. They frequently tell me things like: "My son can't cooperate with other kids"; "My daughter always likes to be boss"; "Jack thinks people are teasing him when they're just joking around"; and "I just wish Julia could see how other kids see her." Some parents admit that they themselves had trouble making friends when they were children. Other parents found making friends easy, but cannot say exactly how they did it. "I don't remember how I made the friends. They were just there."

Raise Your Child's Social IQ offers you the *stepping stones* that your child needs to make and keep friends.

While the skills taught in this book can be discussed and practiced at home, they are learned best while in the company of other children. These techniques were developed as part of the Stepping Stones program, a social skills group therapy training program for children, ranging in age from 4 to 18, and their parents. Although the program was initially designed for therapy groups, the techniques have been modified for use at home by parents. But just as we saw in the therapy setting, social skills are best learned in social settings. So, if your child does not have many social opportunities, it's important that you find or create situations in which your child can practice these skills.

How to Use This Book

This book is divided into ten chapters, each one addressing a particular skill or set of skills that can be practiced with your child in a step-by-step approach. Listed in each chapter are goals that, when mastered, equip each child with the skills necessary to move on to the next chapter.

A quiz will help you determine if your child has already mastered the skills covered in that chapter. It's important to keep in mind as you go through the book that your child will develop skills at his own pace. If you can't check off every skill as "accomplished" by the end of each chapter, don't take it as a sign that your child is not making progress. The checklists are offered only as a guideline.

I suggest that the chapters be read in the order presented because the book begins with basic social skills and progresses in later chapters to more complex skills. However, feel free to focus as much energy and time as necessary on the areas where your child needs the most help.

Remember to introduce the skills one at a time. The shotgun approach will surely overwhelm both you and your child. The Stepping Stones program is designed to concentrate intensely on one problem at a time, thereby ensuring the skill is learned and easily transferred from one situation to another. Each chapter contains tips and techniques as well as practice exercises you can do with your child to make sure he can use his new skills in actual social situations.

It may easily take your child a month or more to acquire the skills laid out in a single chapter. Keep the book by your bed. Pick it up and REFER TO IT OFTEN. You are learning a skill just as your child is, and it takes time to integrate the material. Be patient with yourself and your child as you both are tempted to fall into old patterns of behavior.

For the purpose of simplicity, I have chosen to use the male pronoun "he" throughout the book when generically speaking about a child. Please do not assume this book is only for boys! *Raise Your Child's Social IQ* is appropriate for both girls and boys.

The anecdotes in this book are based on Stepping Stones participants. The names and identifying information have been changed to protect the privacy of the families involved.

So, let's get started!

Chapter One

GETTING
STARTED

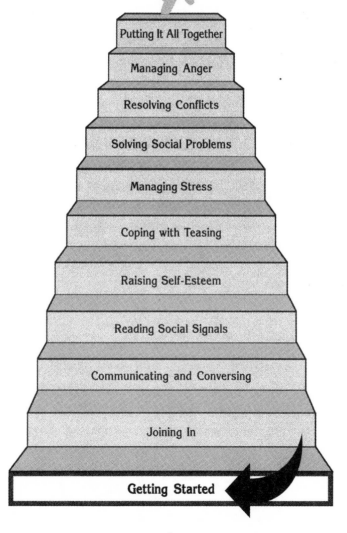

Putting It All Together

Managing Anger

Resolving Conflicts

Solving Social Problems

Managing Stress

Coping with Teasing

Raising Self-Esteem

Reading Social Signals

Communicating and Conversing

Joining In

Getting Started

GOALS ►

In this chapter, you will learn to:

✔ Introduce a new social skill.

✔ Set goals with your child.

✔ Help your child learn good play date behavior.

Madeleine

M adeleine loves to play with other children her age. If she could play after school every day, she would. There are no children in Madeleine's neighborhood, and she attends a private school so her classmates live miles away. This saddens Madeleine greatly. She rarely has the opportunity to play with others. When she does have a playmate, Madeleine becomes so excited that she sometimes doesn't remember how to behave. She tries to take control and doesn't know how to react when her playmate doesn't go along with her plans. Madeleine may cry in frustration at these times or go off to play by herself, leaving her guest alone.

Jeffrey

J effrey, on the other hand, doesn't really like playing with other kids. After he comes home from school and on the weekends, he prefers to play on his own. He likes nothing more than playing a long game of Nintendo or Game Boy. As a matter of fact, Jeffrey could play these games for hours on end if he were allowed to. Jeffrey's parents are concerned about his continuous solitary play. He tells them that he is fine. "I like playing alone." When Jeffrey interacts with other children, he tends to sit back and observe them.

Madeleine and Jeffrey are examples of children who could benefit from improving their social skills. But they will need their parents' help and support to guide them through the skill-building process.

The Parents' Role in Building Social Skills

Some children can't learn social skills on their own—they need help. Your involvement as a parent is essential to help your child learn new skills and use them in a variety of settings. You already help your child to develop social skills by modeling good social skills yourself and by creating situations in which your child can practice. For example, when you invite children over to play or get your child involved in extracurricular activities, you are helping him build social skills. With the use of this book, you are taking it a step further and becoming a social skills coach. As a coach, you and your child are going to practice techniques, games, and exercises that will help your child raise his social IQ.

Skills for Parents

Before you can begin helping your child, you must build your own expertise as a coach. Your new role requires you to wear several different hats, some of which will be unfamiliar to you. The following are procedures you will use regularly in the process of helping your child raise his social IQ.

Setting Goals

▸ **Review chapter goals.**

This book is divided into ten chapters, each of which addresses a specific set of skills to be worked on by your child. At the beginning of each chapter, there is a list of goals for that skill and a quiz that will enable you to assess how much work your child needs in that area.

▸ **Personalize the goals for your child.**

Once you have reviewed the objectives for the chapter, you can personalize the goals for your child. For instance, if you are on Chapter Two working on joining in, you may decide that more than any other skill, your child needs particular help on developing eye contact. In that case, your child's daily, weekly, or monthly goal would be to increase eye contact.

▸ **Put the goal(s) in writing.**

If you sit down with your child and write out a goal, he will take it more seriously than if you only review a goal verbally. It's important to be as specific as possible when setting a goal, and to set only one goal at a time.

When developing a goal with your child, follow
these steps:

 | **Step One** | ***Talk to your child about the need for social skills, and introduce "the skill of the week."***

During a quiet time of the day, discuss with your child the
importance of making friends and getting along with others. An ideal time is when your child is complaining to
you about a social incident with another child. Tell him
you are going to try to help him learn the skills that he
needs to be a better friend. But be careful what you say.
You don't want to emphasize social problems that already
make your child feel badly about himself. Your goal is to
make him feel supported and hopeful. Instead of saying,
"I want to help you make friends," he might respond better if you say, "I want to help you have even *more* friends."

Introduce the skill from the chapter. Review the "Do's"
and "Don'ts" of the skill. You may need to work on a
particular goal for a week, a month, or possibly longer.
These goals are building blocks and each goal should be
met before another is started. Don't worry about the
schedule. Take your time working your way through the
book. Social skills don't develop overnight, they develop
with time and effort.

Step Two | Choose a goal with your child.

You may want your child to stop interrupting others during conversation, but if he doesn't agree or doesn't feel able to meet the goal he will not succeed. Ask your child to choose a social skill goal that appeals to him. You may need to help him come up with ideas. It's best if the goals are specific and measurable. Don't shoot too high. You want to choose a goal that your child will be able to accomplish; otherwise, he will feel defeated. Here are some examples of good and ineffective goals:

Good Goals:	Ineffective Goals:
▸ Susan will interrupt in conversation 50% less this week than last week.	▸ Susan will stop interrupting. (unrealistic goal)
▸ Henry will join a group playing in the neighborhood one time this week.	▸ Henry will make a friend this week. (unrealistic goal)
▸ Jesse will practice one new way to deal with being teased this week.	▸ Jesse will handle teasing better this week. (poorly defined goal)
▸ Matthew will show he is listening (by nodding his head or saying "uh huh") at least once a day this week.	▸ Matthew will be a good listener at school. (too general)
▸ Patty will have 50% fewer temper tantrums this week.	▸ Patty will control her temper. (unrealistic)

Step Three | **Establish a baseline.**

Before you can set an attainable goal, you need to know your child's current level of competence. This step is EXTREMELY IMPORTANT. You may want to skip over it to get right to work on your goals, but don't give in to this temptation!

You will need at least a week to observe your child at home, and perhaps have others observe him at school. Set up a specific time each day to observe your child, and ask his teacher to do the same.

> Before you can set an attainable goal, you need to know your child's current level of competence.

To some degree, when and where your child is observed depends on the goal. For instance, if your child complains that he plays alone every day at recess, the teacher will need to observe him on the playground to see if this is true, and to see how often and for how long he actually plays with others. If he plays by himself daily, your goal clearly will be more modest than if he already plays with others most of the time. If you don't think your child can accomplish a certain goal, set a more realistic one. It's essential that your child feel confident that he can meet the agreed-upon goal. Remember, success breeds success. So, set a goal that is attainable. The confidence your child feels from being successful will prepare him to succeed at the next, more-challenging goal.

Step Four	**Write down all of the elements of the goal.**

Include the "who, what, when, and where" of the goal. Specifically, write down who the goal involves, where the goal will be performed, what the goal is, and by when it is to be accomplished. For example: "Sarah will say hello (what) to Pam (who) tomorrow at lunch (when) in the cafeteria (where)."

Step Five	**Do a "check-in."**

If the goal is a daily one, make sure you check in with your child to see whether the goal was accomplished. Keep track of progress on your written goal sheet (see sample on next page).

Sample Goal Sheet

Goal: Jack will start a conversation with a child in school at least three times in one week.

Monday

Started conversation   ☐ Yes   ☐ No

Conversation starter: _____

With whom: _____

Where did the conversation take place: _____

Tuesday

Started conversation   ☐ Yes   ☐ No

Conversation starter: _____

With whom: _____

Where did the conversation take place: _____

Wednesday

Started conversation   ☐ Yes   ☐ No

Conversation starter: _____

With whom: _____

Where did the conversation take place: _____

Thursday

Started conversation   ☐ Yes   ☐ No

Conversation starter: _____

With whom: _____

Where did the conversation take place: _____

Friday

Started conversation   ☐ Yes   ☐ No

Conversation starter: _____

With whom: _____

Where did the conversation take place: _____

Reward chosen: _____

Child signature: _____

Parent signature: _____

Step Six   *Reward your child for his progress.*

If your child accomplishes his goal, reward him. Your child is working on something that is hard for him. Although the ultimate rewards are self-confidence and better friendships, the rewards you give him now will motivate him to do the hard work of practicing social skills.

Before embarking on the goal, develop a list of possible rewards from which your child can choose if he succeeds. Parental praise and acknowledgment is more important than material rewards. Don't overdo it. Regularly change the rewards to keep them interesting. After the skill is mastered, move on to a new goal. You no longer need to reward for the old goal once it has been achieved, but continue to verbally praise *all* goals accomplished. Don't forget to record progress and reward each newly accomplished goal so that your child does not forget what he is working on.

Possible Rewards:

- ▸ Stickers, stars, or chips which can be traded in for a small toy
- ▸ Time with a parent alone (without siblings)
- ▸ Staying up later at night
- ▸ Extra computer time
- ▸ Choice of dessert
- ▸ Extra TV time
- ▸ Playing a special game
- ▸ Special snack or treat
- ▸ Renting a video

Encouraging the Basics

Often children are unable to manage the details of running a social life. With a little bit of advance planning, you can help make your child's social life more like a playground than a battlefield. The following tips will help:

1. Help your child nurture one or two friendships.

It's more important that your child has one or two very good friends than a slew of acquaintances. The friendship of one child can be just the buffer your child needs to help him deal with the stresses of life. The goal of this book is to help children learn the skills necessary to make a friend. It's not necessary for your child to win popularity contests.

2. Do not overschedule your child with structured extracurricular activities.

It's tempting to join many after-school activities in an attempt to socialize your child. In fact, unstructured play dates are much better environments in which to learn and practice social skills. Also, the stress of running from activity to activity only makes it harder for your child to adequately observe social skills in others.

3. Get involved with community or church activities.

Neighborhood parties and events are wonderful ways for both parents and children to become connected. You often meet compatible families with whom you can set up future outings. Religious youth groups are an excellent

source of potential like-minded f
reluctant to join an organized acti
ment that he try it out at least tw
Sometimes your child might need
sure he knows that he must take
when he does attend so that he doe
failure.

4. **Review social goals with your child prior to social outings.**

For instance, "Tell me, Alice, what are you going to do when you first get to the birthday party?" "I'm going to walk over to where the kids are playing and ask them if I can join." "That's a good idea. Go for it!"

Setting Up the Perfect Play Date

A play date may seem simple and easy to execute, but for the socially challenged child, the play date can be stressful. Try the following ideas to help your child's play date run more smoothly.

Step One | *Invite over one child at a time.*

There is a good reason why "three's a crowd" is such a popular expression. For children with social difficulties, navigating with one other child is hard enough. With the addition of a third, there is a tendency for one to feel left out.

> *Arrange a supervised, time-limited*
> *play date for your child.*

Your child may be unable to spend hours playing with another child. It's too much time for him to negotiate the complicated interactions of play. Instead, set up a play date that is limited in length. Make sure the date ends on a positive note, whenever possible. Children tend to remember more vividly the last 15 minutes of an interaction. If a playmate leaves happy, he is more likely to reciprocate and ask your child over to play next time.

Step Three	*Invite your child's friend to a highly attractive activity.*

Especially if your child is worried about rejection, asking a friend to an enticing activity lessens the likelihood that rejection will take place. If your child has difficulty maintaining conversation, activities such as going ice skating, watching a movie, or touring the zoo do not require prolonged verbal interaction that could tax your socially challenged child.

Step Four	*Set strict limits on TV, computer, and video game time during play dates.*

When your child is playing these games, he is not socializing. These games are very stimulating and addicting, but they do not require a child to interact with others. If your child is on a play date with another child, keep these games off limits for a period of time to give the children a chance to "free play."

Step Five | **Set the stage for playing freely.**

Make your home a safe and comfortable place for children. Have toys available that require two children to play. These do not need to be expensive things. Don't let your child talk you into spending more money in order for him to have fun. These requests may be his way of telling you that he is unsure of himself and how to be a good host to another child.

Step Six | **Review good host behavior.**

Remind your child that the guest gets to choose what he wants to play with. Your child needs to go with the flow. Many children will put up a fuss about this, saying the same rule does not apply when he plays at someone else's house. Commiserate with your child, but still reinforce the "guest chooses" rule.

Step Seven | **Make a list of activities that your child can play when a friend comes over.**

If your child is uncomfortable sharing certain toys, make sure these toys are out of reach when his friend comes over to play.

Sample Activities List:

- ▶ Play tag
- ▶ Build a fort
- ▶ Play a card game
- ▶ Do an art project

Modeling

"Modeling" means demonstrating for your child how to perform a particular behavior. Parents are always modeling social skills, without even knowing it. For many children, this "passive" modeling is sufficient to help them learn what they need to know to get along with others. If you take turns, cooperate with others, go with the flow, and say "please" and "thank you," you are modeling for your child. Throughout this book, you are asked to model the skills being taught. Some of these skills are easy, but for the more challenging skills, even parents may have trouble demonstrating them appropriately. When you reach the chapters on conflict resolution, stress management, and anger control, you will need to pay very close attention to how you model these skills for your child. While you are helping your child, you also may be improving your own behavior.

You will be asked to actively model skills for your child. This means you will demonstrate a skill through role-play. Here's how it works:

▸ You talk through a sample scenario.

▸ Your child observes you.

▸ Your child gives you feedback.

▸ Your child then tries to repeat the skill.

See the following role-play example:

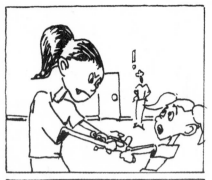

Prompting

There are many opportunities for your child to use his social skills. The problem is that he may not always remember to use them. It's your job to gently, but firmly, remind your child to use his skills. You won't need to prompt him as much "on the scene" if you can anticipate with him social occasions when his skills are going to come in handy. When these situations arise, review social goals with your child prior to the event.

If you are present at a social event, observe your child. After you have given your child ample time to demonstrate a skill, you may need to prompt him. For instance, away from the other kids, Dad could say, "Mike, remember we talked before about taking turns?" or "Remember how we learned to settle arguments?" Be firm when prompting, but don't use an angry tone of voice. This might embarrass your child. Remind your child of the personal goal you have set together. "Brad, remember your goal is to sit at lunch with your friend, Brian." Another way to prompt privately is to discuss a nonverbal cue that only you and your child understand that can be performed in public. For instance, you could pull on your ear to tell your child his voice is too loud.

Practicing/Rehearsing

Practicing social skills is like practicing a musical instrument or a sport. Everyone needs to practice, but different levels of natural talent will require different levels of effort. Children with a lower social IQ are going to require more practice. For many children, the need for consistent rehearsal is even more crucial. You are fortunate if you have a child who can role-play once or twice and then perform the skill in a natural setting. Often times, children need to role-play, then practice in a real-life situation, and then role-play again. This cycle could repeat itself ten or twelve times before the skill is more automatic. Rehearse as much as necessary. It's the practice that actually gives your child the confidence he needs to perform the skill.

Taking Baby Steps

It can be frustrating to teach children social skills. Just when you think they have mastered one thing, you see that they are still struggling in other areas. It's essential for you to notice and praise your child's brave attempts at learning these skills. Some forms of praise are much more effective than others. Following are tips for effective praise:

Tips for Praising

▶ Praise effort, not necessarily outcome.

▶ Praise anytime you witness a skill performed.

▶ Praise the behavior. Refrain from generalities.

▶ Praise your child twice for every criticism you offer.

If you are accustomed to giving your child negative feed-back for misbehavior, instead try to praise your child for good behavior.

Praise and encouragement, more than anything else, will help your child develop social skills. Look for oppor-tunities to praise your child.

Encouraging Social Skills

Keep in mind the following guidelines as you embark on this program. Following them will assist you in helping your child transfer his new skills to real-life situations.

General Guidelines

▸ Review the tips and techniques in this book, and practice them one by one with your child.

▸ Observe, practice, praise, and enhance social skills as you witness them.

▸ Track specific goals on a daily/weekly basis.

▸ Look for small signs of progress and encourage those behaviors.

Ways to Help Your Child Practice Social Skills

▸ Role-play social skills at home.

▸ Videotape or audiotape your child at home. Review the tapes with your child. This lets your child see himself as others see him.

▸ Find ways to incorporate this book's exercises into your existing activities, such as dinnertime, car rides, and bedtime routines.

▸ Involve siblings when possible. These relationships can offer a safer arena in which to practice new social skills. Siblings offer a rich interpersonal environment in which to resolve conflicts, practice problem solving, try new anger control techniques, and learn to deal with teasing.

Changing Your Child's Environment to Enhance Social Skills

▸ Involve teachers and guidance counselors in reinforcing specific goals. The use of check-off sheets by teachers can give day-to-day feedback on progress, as well as encourage accountability and consistency for your child.

▸ When necessary, act as an advocate for your child. Sometimes it's necessary to change his environment to reinforce newly learned skills. Peers can be unforgiving and unwilling to let go of old ways of viewing your child. Switching classrooms or schools (in cases of extreme discomfort) may be necessary. Remember that poor social skills will follow your child into a new environment, so don't make drastic changes until he has acquired new skills.

Now that I've covered the basics, you're ready to start working on specific social skills. Good luck!

Chapter Two

JOINING IN

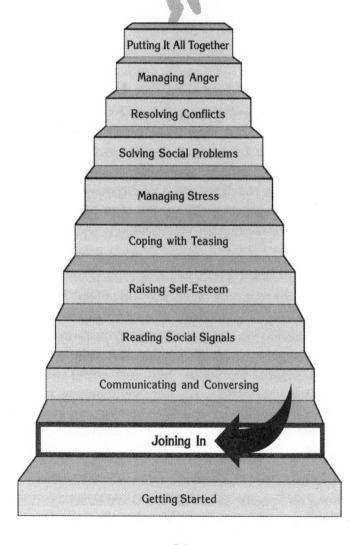

Putting It All Together

Managing Anger

Resolving Conflicts

Solving Social Problems

Managing Stress

Coping with Teasing

Raising Self-Esteem

Reading Social Signals

Communicating and Conversing

Joining In

Getting Started

GOALS ▸

In this chapter, you will learn how to help your child:

- ✔ Join in with others.
- ✔ Know when it's okay to join the group.
- ✔ Watch for the friendly face.
- ✔ Make a good first impression.
- ✔ "Go with the flow" of a group.

Max

Max is nine. He has just moved to the East Coast from Los Angeles because his father took a new job. Max has a hard time adjusting every time Dad gets a new job and moves the family. It's not easy for Max to make friends; he doesn't warm up to people quickly. At recess, for instance, Max would really like to play with the other kids, but he doesn't know how to join in. He tends to stand off to the side and watch the others play. Max is not rejected by his peers, but he is not included either. Until recently, Max's mother would request a list of phone numbers of Max's classmates from his teachers. She then would arrange his play dates. This worked very well when Max was in first and second grade. But now, Max is getting too old for her to do this for him. When Mom asks him for names and telephone numbers of friends at his new school, Max can't come up with anyone. When Mom asks Max whom he plays with at recess, he says that he plays by himself. Max isn't invited over to anyone's house, and in the last few years, he's been invited to very few birthday parties. Mom is becoming concerned about Max's social life. Max complains that he *doesn't have any friends and that he doesn't know what to say to the other kids at recess. Mom wonders how she can teach Max the skills he needs to join in.*

Jennifer

*J*ennifer, *on the other hand, doesn't have a shy bone in her body. She is a bright, friendly ten-year-old girl with a terrific sense of humor. Adults love her, particularly her teachers who think she is quite funny and entertaining. She'll start a conversation with anybody who will talk to her. Jennifer's problem is that she pays no attention to whether the group of kids she approaches want to talk to her. Her peers see her as pushy and intrusive. She has no idea why groups of children move away when she approaches. She is friendly, but does not realize that she comes on too strong. Jennifer is beginning to notice that her classmates are rejecting her because they whisper about her and call her names behind her back. Jennifer's dad thinks his daughter is wonderful, but even he notices when he picks her up at the bus stop that the other girls avoid her. Jennifer's parents want to help their daughter make a good impression on others so she doesn't continue to be rejected and lose her wonderful spirit.*

Joining in is one of the most important skills for kids to learn because the first impression they make is often how they will be judged by their peers. Children are frequently exposed to new situations, such as moving to a new school, or joining a sports team, which require them to smoothly join an unfamiliar group. Children who have difficulty joining in usually fall into one of two types. They either stand to the side and observe, unable to make the move to join the group, or they join too abruptly or aggressively, alienating the other group members.

The Joining In Quiz

Ask yourself the following questions to determine if your child might need help learning how to join a group and make a good first impression:

☐ Does your child easily approach a new group of children?

☐ Does your child wait for an appropriate break in the conversation before saying something?

☐ Does your child join a conversation smoothly by asking a question that relates to what's going on?

☐ Does your child look others directly in the eye when speaking?

☐ Does your child stop and check out a group before joining?

☐ Can your child "go with the flow" of a group?

If you answered *yes* to all of these questions, then you can just skip over this chapter. If you answered *no* to some of them, it would be worthwhile for you to continue reading and try some of the exercises in this chapter.

Joining In

Joining a group is not easy. Your child may enter group situations inappropriately or awkwardly, unaware of how his behavior impacts the group. The following steps can help your child learn strategies to join in more effectively.

Step One | **Wait. Watch. Listen.**

Max can handle this part. He's very good at taking his time to check out the group he wants to join. Max watches what the group is doing and figures out a strategy for joining. He is good at sizing up the group to see if it's one he wants to join. His problem is that he can't take the next step. Jennifer, on the other hand, needs help sizing up the situation. The first step to joining in is to take a few minutes to check out the group—wait, watch, and listen. Jennifer needs to be more observant before she jumps in.

I once worked with a fourth-grader named Tommy who behaved a lot like Max. Tommy could recognize the popular kids a mile away. The problem was that although Tommy pursued these popular kids, they didn't want to play with him. In each new town to which his family moved throughout his childhood, Tommy was routinely rejected by the popular crowd, leaving him feeling pretty badly about himself. It wasn't until Tommy realized that there were other kids in his class with whom he had more in common that he began to be accepted. He stopped trying to join in with kids who weren't receptive and was much happier as a result.

Review the following chart with your child to help him understand how to choose appropriate groups to join.

Do's	Don'ts
Do join groups that are:	Don't join groups that are:
▸ Playing safely	▸ Playing unsafely
▸ Playing cooperatively	▸ Playing uncooperatively
▸ Playing fairly	▸ Fighting
▸ Following the rules	▸ Wild
▸ Taking turns	▸ Mean to people who want to join in
▸ Smiling and friendly	

Step Two | *Find the friendly face.*

Once your child determines that the group is safe to join, he still has to take some time to observe. Try practicing with your child watching other children at the playground. Help your child pick out the children who appear more open and friendly—the ones your child will have an easier time approaching. For Max, sizing up a large group of children felt overwhelming. He just could not break down the group into smaller, more manageable parts. When he tried to join the mass of kids, he would freeze with anxiety. But when Max learned to search for the one or two kids who smiled and looked approachable, he had an easier time joining the group at his own pace.

It's often the case that the children on the periphery of a group are friendlier. Kids who are the leaders of a group may not necessarily be the most welcoming. If your child tells you he has no friends and everyone teases him or leaves him out, try to help him narrow his perspective. When a few kids are being mean, your child may feel as if the whole world is against him. If you must, systematically go through a list of every classmate until you find one that is pleasant to your child. Then, help your child target that classmate for friendship. Encourage your child to slowly develop a relationship with that child by initiating conversations and finding common interests. Then encourage him to exchange telephone numbers and invitations to play.

| Step Three | *Figure out what to say ahead of time.* |

Practice joining-in questions with your child. For instance, "Can I join?" or "Do you want to play?" Some children may not want to say anything when they join in. Instead, they're more comfortable going with the flow of the group without saying a word. For example, if a group is playing tag, your child may simply begin running from the person who is "it." He should make sure to follow the rules of the game and just go with the flow.

It's not really necessary for a child to introduce himself to a group. This actually may interrupt the flow of the group. Names can be exchanged later after the group gets to know each other a bit through the games they're playing. Children who have very good social skills intuitively know how to join in unobtrusively.

Step Four	**Watch yourself carefully.**

There is a fine line between watching yourself so carefully that you become self-conscious, like Max, and not observing yourself at all, like Jennifer. This is a tricky balance for kids of junior high-school age, in particular, who become vulnerable to self-consciousness. These kids watch themselves so carefully that they feel incapable of making any move at all. They worry that anything they say will be judged by their peers. If your child is like this, don't emphasize self-observation, just talk about the need to be careful.

For others, like Jennifer, self-observation is very important. Children who have impulse-control problems have trouble thinking before acting. These children need to slow down and understand how others view them. It's helpful to review appropriate behaviors with your child before a new situation. Remind him of the three guidelines for making a good first impression:

- ▶ Stay calm.
- ▶ Wait your turn.
- ▶ Go with the flow.

After each new social situation, check in with your child to see how he did.

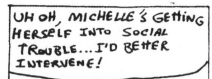

| **Step Five** | *Role-play joining in.* |

Role-playing allows children to practice skills before they need to use them in real-life situations. Your child has the chance to practice behaviors and receive positive feedback from you. While you role-play, focus on potentially troublesome social scenarios and offer solutions to the problems. Here's how to role-play:

1. Discuss the skill to be mastered.

Talk with your child about the skill he needs to work on. For instance, Max's parents may want to talk with their son about his problems joining in. They should get a clear understanding of the problems and what issues get in Max's way.

2. Rehearse the steps.

Verbally rehearse the steps necessary to master the skill. For example, if Max is trying to learn how to join in at recess, his parents need to review with him the steps necessary to achieve that goal:

- ▸ Wait. Watch. Listen.
- ▸ Find the friendly face.
- ▸ Figure out what to say ahead of time.
  Actually come up with the line Max is going to use. For example, "Can I join in?"
- ▸ Join in.

3. Set the stage.

Create the scene where this skill is going to be used. In this case, since Max tries to join in at recess, the role-play can take place during recess. Pretend there is a group of children playing tag that he wants to join. When you role-play, the stage will be set for the action to take place. Create different scenes depending on where your child commonly runs into difficulty—for example, at a neighborhood playground, at a friend's house, at a birthday party, and so on.

4. Model the skill for your child.

Show your child exactly what he should do. In Max's case, his mother may decide to play the role of Max at recess. She will go through the steps outlined above, and join the group appropriately. She models for Max exactly how this process can succeed.

5. Have your child practice the skill.

It's important that your child knows all these steps before role-playing. You may need to review the steps or even write them down. Also review the roles of all the "players." For instance, if Mom is going to play a "Friendly Person" at the playground, review how she will respond. If Dad is going to play a "Rejecting Child," review ahead of time how your child is going to respond.

Practice the skills, gradually increasing the degree of difficulty for your child. Initially, the group of children he joins can be accepting. Later, they can become more challenging to join, perhaps even rejecting your child. Practice with your child ways to handle rejecting situations—perhaps he just walks away

> Practice the skills, gradually increasing the degree of difficulty for your child.

and finds another group to play with, or perhaps he says to himself, "Oh well, maybe next time."

Role-playing is a very useful exercise for practicing any of the skills discussed in this book. The steps remain the same, but the skills themselves change.

Another valuable practice technique is "role reversal." In this exercise, you freeze the action and in the middle of a role-play, allow your child to take on the role of "the other." I have found this method very effective for children who have a hard time seeing how their behavior affects others. When they are given the chance to view themselves through the eyes of the other, it's amazing how eye-opening the experience can be for them.

6. Give positive feedback.

Positive feedback is an excellent way to reinforce skills. Feedback can take the form of suggestions, coaching, praise, and support. Here are some suggestions for giving feedback:

- ▸ Begin with a positive statement: "Jennifer, I like the way you spoke in a calm, clear voice."

- ▸ *Never* make discouraging statements: "They'll never want to play with you if you join in like that!"

- ▸ Give criticism in a constructive way: "You might want to smile next time." "Rather than looking at the floor, try looking at their eyes."

- ▸ Remember that it's much easier to give negative feedback than positive, but positive feedback is much more effective and far less damaging.

Joining In Games and Exercises

1. The Do's and Don'ts

Review with your child the following Do's and Don'ts of joining in. Ask your child to come up with additions to these lists.

Do's:	Don'ts:
▸ Watch others.	▸ Don't tease others.
▸ Go with the flow of the group. Try to do what they're doing, and at the speed they're doing it.	▸ Don't brag about yourself.
	▸ Don't criticize others.
▸ Find common interests and talk about them.	▸ Don't take charge and try to control the behavior of other children.
▸ Ask a question that shows interest. This is a good conversation icebreaker.	
	▸ Don't interrupt others.
▸ Address your first question to the child who is smiling, who seems open to hearing from you.	▸ Don't stand too close or too far away from other children.
	▸ Don't disrupt a game.
▸ Join a group that appears friendly, and where the children are playing safely and fairly.	▸ Don't join others who make it clear to you that they don't want you to play with them.

2. Meet and Greet

Create a "Meet and Greet" diary with your child to chart his progress.

Was there a group of children you wanted to join this week?

☐ Yes   ☐ No

Describe the situation:

_____

_____

_____

_____

_____

_____

_____

Write down the Do's you used:

1._____

2._____

3._____

4._____

Positive comments from parents or teachers:

_____

_____

_____

_____

3. Role-Play

▸ Role-play with your child, allowing him to play the role of the "joiner" first, then the "joinee."

▸ Have him practice by attempting to join in a game of cards or catch.

▸ Involve siblings in the role-play wherever possible.

▸ Try to focus on the Do's of good social skills.

▸ Praise your child for appropriate behavior.

Chapter Three

COMMUNICATING
AND CONVERSING

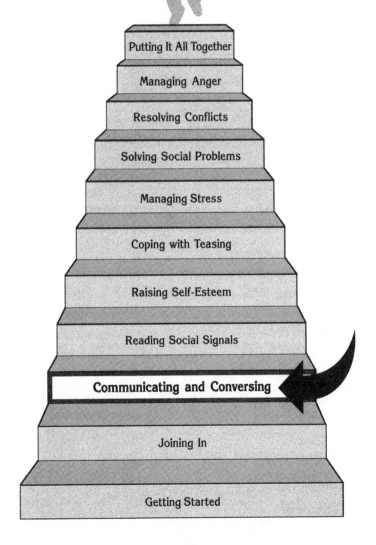

Putting It All Together

Managing Anger

Resolving Conflicts

Solving Social Problems

Managing Stress

Coping with Teasing

Raising Self-Esteem

Reading Social Signals

Communicating and Conversing

Joining In

Getting Started

GOALS ▶

In this chapter, you will learn how to help your child:

- ✔ Make consistent eye contact with others.
- ✔ Develop active listening skills.
- ✔ Ask appropriate questions when there is a pause in the conversation.
- ✔ Say things that express interest in the other person.
- ✔ Experience a comfortable give-and-take in conversation.
- ✔ Maintain a conversation.
- ✔ Respect personal body space.
- ✔ Use a clear and pleasant tone of voice.

Sally

*M*om is concerned about her daughter, Sally. While Sally usually makes a good first impression when she meets other children, it's extremely hard for her to develop lasting friendships. Mom wants to help her daughter develop deeper connections with others, but she doesn't know how to help. On the surface, Sally appears to get along quite well with other children. She is an outgoing and confident eight-year-old. She has no trouble going up to unfamiliar children, asking to join them, and jumping right in. Sally plays actively and enthusiastically. Children are immediately drawn to her energy and good-natured spirit.

For Sally, joining in the game is easy; maintaining friendships is not. Within minutes, it becomes clear that as much as Sally likes to play, she likes to play **her** way. In her easygoing manner, she shifts the play towards something she'd like to do. With little regard for those around her, she begins telling everyone the rules of her new game. She assumes that the other children will join her. When they don't, she becomes confused and frustrated. It doesn't occur to Sally to check in with her new friends to see what they'd like to do. She doesn't think to ask questions that will help her understand their wishes. Sally doesn't hear her peers' protests to her enthusiastic ideas. Instead, she just does whatever she wants. Instead of ending up with a group to play with, Sally's behavior usually results in her walking away in frustration, or the other children distancing themselves from her.

Will

Will's dad is a quiet computer programmer who generally keeps to himself at work. He interacts with others only when approached, and generally is more comfortable engaging in solitary activities. His twelve-year-old son, Will, has similar tendencies. Will has difficulties with conversation, but unlike Sally, Will's behavior doesn't result in rejection or avoidance by other children. Instead, Will experiences social disconnection. Will approaches groups and new people tentatively. He tends to be an observer rather than an active participant. Will's mom has worked diligently over the years on helping her son feel more comfortable joining in with groups of children. An outgoing person herself, Mom helped Will by frequently exposing him to social group activities. But now that Will is older, she is less able to develop his social life for him. She can't pick up the phone and call neighborhood children to come over and play, as she used to.

Will is comfortable in a group only when he is required to speak very little, such as when he's playing computer games or chess. Will's troubles arise when he's required to keep a

*conversation going. He just can't seem to think of what to say
next. He answers questions with a simple yes or no. As a result, the conversations tend to die out. Rather than turning the
conversation around and asking questions himself, Will waits
for questions to be asked of him. Will has just a few friends
with whom he hangs out and plays computer games, but they
rarely communicate with each other. He tells his parents that
he is satisfied with his friendships and likes spending time
alone. In reality, he'd like to be able to maintain and deepen
conversations with others. Dad feels that his wife overreacts to
Will's conversational style. After all, Dad himself is very similar to Will and is doing fine, both personally and professionally. But Mom is worried that Will is not learning the skills he
needs to get along with others in life.*

Parental Social Styles and Temperaments

It's obvious that Will and Sally are very different children.
Although they both have difficulties communicating effectively with their peers, their different temperaments
cause these struggles to surface in different ways. Before
you can help your child develop good conversation skills,
it's essential to clearly understand both your own and your
child's social style and temperament. For instance, you
may be less inclined to intervene if his way of relating to
others is similar to your own, even if this style has not
been especially successful for you. Likewise, you may
have the tendency to overreact to your child if his social
style is very different from yours, even if your child's style
works perfectly well for him. In Will's case, for example,
Dad is introverted, independent, and socially detached.

So it's not surprising that he isn't concerned with Will's behavior, while his outgoing, extroverted wife is very concerned.

The Good Conversation Skills Quiz

Take the following quiz to determine if your child has real conversational challenges. Observe whether your child exhibits these behaviors regularly in interactions with other children:

☐ Does your child look into another's eyes when speaking?

☐ Does your child actively listen when spoken to?

☐ Does your child allow others a chance to speak and be heard?

☐ Does your child speak in a calm, pleasant tone of voice?

☐ Does your child show interest in another person by asking questions?

☐ Does your child keep his body still when speaking with another person?

☐ Does your child often initiate conversations with others?

☐ Does your child talk on the phone with other children?

☐ Are your child's statements and questions relevant to the topic being discussed?

☐ Does your child use appropriate body language with others?

☐ Does your child use appropriate language in conversation?

☐ Does your child make supportive statements to others while he is talking, such as: "That's great!"; "Wow!"; and "Yeah!"?

If you answered *yes* to all of these questions, then you can just skip over this chapter. If you answered *no* to some of them, it would be worthwhile for you to continue reading and try some of the exercises in this chapter.

How To Be a Good Communicator

Make Good Eye Contact

If we look more closely at Sally's situation, we can see that part of what makes Sally unaware of the negative responses she's getting from her peers is that she simply isn't looking at them. She is so focused on her own desires that she does not stop to look at her friends. If Sally could look at them straight in the eyes, she'd be more likely to see their looks of disapproval. She then might be able to hear their protests and change her behavior accordingly. I'll talk more in Chapter Four about reading social signals—facial expressions, body language, and social responses of others. Making good eye contact is a precursor to reading social signals. It's impossible to understand the cues others give you without looking them in the eye and "tuning in" to their feelings and experiences.

Eye contact is one of the best ways to make another person feel special. In the adult world, people who don't look you straight in the eye are viewed as untrustworthy, lacking in self-confidence, or self-absorbed. In a child's world, kids view peers who don't look at them as distracted, disconnected, or disinterested. In my training groups with children, we periodically "freeze" the discussion to see which children are looking at the speaker.

When we ask the speaker which children he feels are listening, he inevitably names those who are looking at him. Children are drawn to those who make them feel good about themselves by looking at them and listening.

Good eye contact is the foundation upon which more subtle and complex communication skills are built. It is the first step in the give-and-take required for a successful conversation.

Tips for Developing Good Eye Contact

▸ Make sure your child is looking at you when you are speaking to him.

▸ Choose a code word with your child, such as "Eyes!" or "Look!", to remind him to look at the other person. This code word acts as a prompt without embarrassing your child.

▸ Remember to verbally praise your child when you see him engaging in good eye contact. For example, "Boy, Charlie, I feel so good when you look at me when we're talking."

▸ Play the "freeze" game at the dinner table to point out those who are paying attention and those who are not.

Practice "Active" Listening

What do I mean by "active listening?" This is not just ordinary listening. Active listening lets the speaker know he is being listened to. Active listening is an extremely important component of effective communication.

If we look again at Will's situation, we see that he listens to others passively, not actively. He waits for his friends to engage him in conversation. Although Will does a good job with some of the components of active listening—such as looking at the person, keeping his body still, and waiting for a pause to speak—he doesn't do the things that show interest in the other person that keep the conversation going.

It's easy to teach children to use active listening words in conversation. I remember once working in a group with a ten-year-old named David. As good a listener as David was, he had trouble showing physically that he was, in fact, listening. His eye contact was good, but his facial expression was flat and disinterested. It took us many attempts before we came up with some solutions. David chose two strategies to show us he was listening: nodding his head with affirmation (not often, but often enough) and saying, "Uh huh." These relatively simple, active responses came in very handy for David. The other children in the group agreed that they felt much more connected to David after he began using these new signals.

Checklist for Active Listening

☐ Look at the person and have a pleasant look on your face.

☐ Keep your hands and body still.

☐ Allow the person to speak without interrupting.

☐ Periodically make sounds or say things that express interest in what the speaker is saying, such as: "Hmmm"; "Oh"; "Uh huh"; or "Yeah."

☐ When there is a pause, ask a question or make a statement that relates to the subject matter.

Will is going to have to go further than just making sounds that express interest. He's going to need to actively keep the conversation moving forward. Generally, as much as children like to talk about themselves, they need urging from the listener to continue talking about a subject. It's important that there be a give-and-take in the conversation. It's like a game of catch. The speaker throws the ball to the listener. The listener catches the ball by using active listening words. The listener then throws back the ball by asking a question that expresses interest, or by making a statement that shows understanding. The speaker returns the ball by continuing with the conversation on the same subject. In order to have a satisfying game of catch, the ball needs to go back and forth more than a couple of times before the game stops. It's the same with conversation. A conversation flows when the give-and-take goes back and forth several times. So Will must do more than just listen to have a satisfying conversation—he needs to ask a question or make a statement that will keep the conversation going.

Your child may be genuinely disinterested and some-
what self-absorbed, so he may not have the desire to continue the conversation. "I don't care about what he's saying, so why should I ask him questions?" "He's boring."
Naturally, you have a greater challenge with a child who
lacks interest in and empathy for other children. For this
child, it's crucial to help him understand that you can't
make a friend without being a friend. You must emphasize the feelings of others by saying things like, "How would
you feel if . . . ?" This culture values independence and
self-determination in children. But these traits can lead
to a decrease in your child's ability to identify and relate
to the needs and feelings of others. Independence and
connection are not mutually exclusive concepts. Help
your child value the opinions and desires of others so that
he can develop lasting friendships and significant relationships with others.

Active Listening with Will and Sally

Will falls into the category of child who is interested, but just doesn't know how to keep things going. He genuinely cannot think of what to say next. I have found it helpful to have children silently ask themselves the question, "What comes next?" when a child speaks to them. For instance, let's say John comes up to Will and excitedly says, "Hey, Will, I scored the only goal in soccer today!" Will might just shrug his shoulders, say "Oh," or do nothing at all. But if he stops and thinks to himself, "What might I say to keep things going?" or "What comes next?", he could say, "That's great! When's your next game?" or "Wow! Is soccer your favorite sport?" or "You must be good in soccer." Any of those responses would encourage John to continue. Let's say John responds, "Soccer is my favorite sport. What's yours?" Will could answer, "I like baseball." Then, when Will thinks to himself, "What comes next?", he could respond with, "John, do you play any baseball?" In this way, Will not only is able to keep the conversation going, but he is also able to deepen the conversation. He can even make a game out of it to see how many times he can go back and forth before "dropping the ball."

Sally has a different challenge. Unlike Will, who might listen indefinitely to another person as long as the speaker doesn't require anything of him, Sally struggles with the give-and-take in a conversation because she's all take and very little give. Sally monopolizes her conversations without regard for the listener. Sally's style is much more impulsive than Will's. She can't wait until others respond before she interrupts and blurts out what she wants to say. Waiting for the pause in a conversation is excruciating for her. Part of the reason Sally is rejected by other children is because she already has moved on to the next idea before others have had a chance to respond to the previous one. This makes her peers feel discounted. Sally needs to slow down and think before speaking so that she gives herself the time to listen and take in what another child is saying. For her, waiting for the pause before speaking will be her biggest challenge.

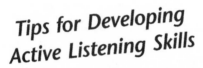

Tips for Developing Active Listening Skills

▶ Use active listening responses when you talk with your child. Make sure when your child speaks to you that you respond with statements and questions that show interest. Your child will learn from you through this modeling method.

▶ Set up a "star chart." Give your child a star every time you see him using active listening techniques.

▶ Practice role-playing with your child. Children love playing the role of somebody else. See how long he can keep the conversation going.

Use a Clear, Pleasant Tone of Voice

If your child speaks with a garbled or overly loud voice, you may want to have his hearing checked to make sure there isn't a physical problem. If his hearing is fine, then it becomes your task to help your child learn to modulate his tone of voice. I can remember quite clearly when my own son was six years old that he had little awareness of how loud his voice was and how gruff it sounded. I had to help him become more aware of how his voice sounded to others.

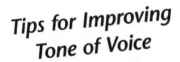

Tips for Improving Tone of Voice

▶ Videotape or audiotape your child in action. Play it back and let your child hear himself through others' ears. He might be very surprised at how he sounds.

▶ Gently remind your child to use an indoor voice, not an outdoor playground voice, when he's inside the house.

▶ Reward your child for every hour his voice level remains low.

▶ Put a mark on your child's hand or on a piece of paper every time his voice is inappropriately loud. At a certain number, the marks translate into loss of privileges. (I prefer using rewards whenever possible, but sometimes quick negative reinforcement can be powerful and effective.)

Respect Another Person's Body Space

Some of the children I see at my office have a hard time recognizing where their bodies end and others' begin. Like puppy dogs with loose and floppy bodies, these children appear to lack awareness of how intrusive it can be when they stand too close to somebody. This behavior could be the result of developmental issues. After all, we don't mind it at all when children who are three or four years old cuddle with each other and bump into each other. They haven't developed the controls yet to stop themselves, and we think their affection for others is endearing. However, we think it is less cute when older children hug and kiss or stand too close to us. This is especially true for boys—if they get too close, they are usually rebuffed and pushed away. Notice when another child backs away from your child. He is likely doing this because his personal space has been invaded.

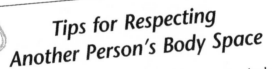

Tips for Respecting Another Person's Body Space

▸ Ask your child to stand in the center of a hula hoop or draw a three-foot circle on the ground around your child. Let him experience how far away he should be from others when talking to them.

▸ Discourage your elementary school-aged child from being affectionate with strangers, including other children.

▸ Help your child recognize the difference between appropriate and inappropriate touching.

Communication Games and Exercises

1. The Do's and Don'ts

Review with your child the Do's and Don'ts of communication. Post the list in a central place in your house. Review them periodically and positively reinforce the good behaviors your child performs. Ask your child to come up with other items to add to the lists.

Do's:	Don'ts:
▸ Wait for a pause before you speak.	▸ Don't "hog" the conversation.
▸ Ask appropriate questions.	▸ Don't change the subject too quickly.
▸ Use a clear and pleasant voice.	▸ Don't interrupt others when they're speaking.
▸ Look the other person straight in the eye.	
▸ Make active listening statements.	

2. The Story Game

Tell a story together with your child, taking turns. You begin. When you stop, it's your child's turn to continue the story. It's important that your child wait his turn before he speaks, and that his part of the story connect to the piece of the story you just told.

3. The Conversation Game

Give your child the opportunity to have a conversation with you and your family. The dinner table can be a good place to play this game. Place a container in the center of the table. The goal of the game is for the family to earn more than 25 coins. A family member begins a conversation. Using coins as rewards, place two coins in the container for every relevant question that is asked following the opening statement. Place one coin in the container for every statement made that is relevant. A coin is removed from the container each time someone does not wait for a pause to speak, or when the subject is changed suddenly. Allow the whole family to play.

4. The TV Talk Show Game

Allow your child to interview you as if he were a TV talk show host. If you can videotape the interview, that's even better. The host of the talk show has three goals.

Host's Goals:	Guest's Goals:
▸ Help make your guest feel more comfortable by using active-listening techniques. ▸ Ask questions of your guest that show interest. ▸ Share information about yourself that relates to your guest's topic.	▸ Answer the host's questions politely. ▸ Stay focused on the topic. ▸ Use active-listening techniques.

Now swap roles and interview your child so he can experience both sides.

5. The Conversation Journal

Develop a weekly conversation journal that tracks and reinforces positive interactions. You can reward your child with stickers, points, or stars that can be traded in for privileges. A communication journal might look like this:

Describe the conversation you had.

_____

_____

_____

Did you try to use the conversation skills you practiced with your parents?

_____

_____

_____

What skills did you think about using?

_____

_____

_____

What skills did you actually use?

_____

_____

_____

How did it work? (not at all, a little, a lot)

_____

_____

_____

6. The Reflective Listening Game

Play the Reflective Listening game. This game is a very challenging one that may feel a bit unnatural to play. The point of the game is to exercise your listening muscles. You're not expected to actually listen like this in everyday conversation!

Family member A	Family member B
▸ Family member A begins a conversation. For instance, "How was your day at school today?"	▸ Before he responds, family member B must reflect back what family member A just said. "You want to know how my day was. My teacher yelled at me in front of the class because I forgot to do my home-work. How was your day?"
▸ Family member A responds, "You want to know how my day was. And you had a bad day because your teacher yelled at you. I'm sorry your day was so bad. My day was uneventful."	▸ Family member B responds, "Your day was uneventful. Thanks for your sympathy about my day."

You can reward your family members for good reflective listening.

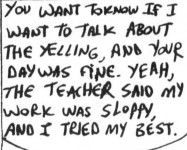

7. The "What Comes Next?" Game

Play the "What Comes Next?" game. This game will help your child deepen a conversation.

▸ A family member brings up a topic of conversation.

▸ Your child must then think of a comment or question to ask which relates to the topic and will keep the conversation going.

▸ This continues like a game of catch until the topic of conversation has been exhausted.

▸ You can earn a reward for each comment or question.

Chapter Four

READING
SOCIAL SIGNALS

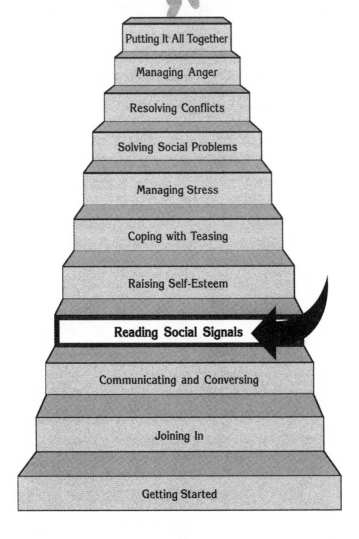

Putting It All Together

Managing Anger

Resolving Conflicts

Solving Social Problems

Managing Stress

Coping with Teasing

Raising Self-Esteem

Reading Social Signals

Communicating and Conversing

Joining In

Getting Started

GOALS ▸

In this chapter, you will learn how to help your child:

✓ Recognize and acknowledge the feelings of others.

✓ Read the body language of others.

✓ Read the facial expressions of others.

✓ Empathize with others.

✓ React appropriately to "on purpose" vs. "by accident" behavior.

✓ Stop a behavior when asked.

Andy

A ndy is an eleven-year-old sixth grader. Andy's parents are concerned about how their son will interact with his peers when he goes to junior high school next year. Andy has a few friends in the neighborhood that he's known for a long time. He trusts them and gets along well with them. But these friends attend a nearby parochial school. Andy comes home from his public school and frequently complains that other kids trip him in the hallway. "They're always bumping into me," he says. "Next time I'm going to just shove them back." Andy's parents listen to their son and empathize with him, but they feel pretty helpless about what to do. They finally decide to contact Andy's teacher. She denies seeing anybody pick on Andy, but she does acknowledge that sometimes Andy overreacts to insignificant slights. If somebody pokes him in the side in a benign, joking way, Andy takes it seriously and gets angry. His teacher *is concerned that if Andy continues to overreact to minor affronts, the kids will begin to see him either as a weak target and tease him, or as a bully and avoid him altogether.*

Lauren

The kids in Lauren's third-grade class call her "clueless." Lauren says really goofy things out loud in class, such as that she is a princess from a foreign land and a boy in fourth grade is her prince. She says she wants to marry this boy and that she's going to kiss him. When the other kids roll their eyes at her, she doesn't notice. Instead, she sees only the one or two kids that are laughing. Lauren thinks the gigglers are laughing with her, not at her, so she continues telling her silly stories to get them to laugh more. Her teacher warns her to settle down. Lauren isn't really paying attention to the teacher, she's paying attention to the giggles and whispers of *her peers, hoping that they like her stories. So she continues to tell tall tales, becoming louder and more dramatic. The other kids tell her to be quiet. The teacher restricts Lauren from going to recess because she has to complete the schoolwork she just missed by fooling around. Lauren doesn't understand why she's being punished and why the kids in class don't like her, no matter how hard she tries to please them. This is the fourth time in a month she is sent home with a disciplinary note. Lauren's parents are frustrated with Lauren's problem. They try to explain to her how she should behave, but she doesn't seem to understand.*

Lauren and Andy are examples of children who have difficulty reading and understanding social signals. Children who are socially competent are capable of regularly scanning their environment for clues that will guide their social actions. These kids can easily tune in to what is happening around them and figure out what is required of them. They generally experience a wide range of emotions and are able to express and label complex feelings appropriately. This skill makes it easier for them to empathize with others.

The Reading Social Signals Quiz

Use the following quiz to determine if your child has difficulty reading social signals:

☐ Does your child approach others in a cooperative manner, considering the feelings of others?

☐ When another child asks your child to stop doing something, does he stop?

☐ When your child sees another child give him a dirty look, does your child's behavior change in response? For instance, if your child is yelling and receives a dirty look, does he stop yelling?

☐ Can your child follow suggestions of others in a group activity?

☐ Is your child a good sport?

☐ Does your child react to accidental behavior appropriately? (Or does he usually think it's deliberate?)

☐ When told about an upsetting event by a friend, would your child say something sympathetic, such as, "Oh, that's too bad"?

If you answered *yes* to all of these questions, then you can just skip over this chapter. If you answered *no* to some of them, it would be worthwhile for you to continue reading and try some of the exercises in this chapter.

Empathy

The ability to empathize is a highly complex skill. Empathy is defined as the capacity to feel and think what another feels and thinks by observing his verbal and nonverbal cues.

Checklist for Good Empathy

☐ Concentrate on what the person is saying.

☐ Notice the behavior of the other person and try to understand what is being communicated by that behavior.

☐ Imagine the feelings of the other person.

☐ Respond appropriately.

Yikes! This may seem like a pretty complicated process. It's no wonder that so many children (and adults) struggle with it.

In Lauren's case, she reads her classmates' cues as if they were in a foreign language. As much as Lauren would like the kids to like her, and as much as she tries to pay attention to social cues at school, her behavior, instead, is out of whack and downright disruptive. Andy, on the other hand, has the ability to tune in to others when he trusts them. The problem is that he doesn't trust anyone at his school and tends to believe the worst of those around him.

Developing Empathy

The following is a series of steps for you to help your child develop empathy. This is one area where specific examples and modeling appropriate behavior are extremely effective.

Step One	*Pay attention to social matters in your child's life.*

Begin by getting a clear picture of your child's social world. Ask specific questions about your child's friends and acquaintances. "Who sits across from you at lunch?" "What did you talk about with Susie today?" "What do you like to play at recess?" These questions indicate to your child that social matters are important and interpersonal relationships are worth developing and maintaining.

Step Two	*Prompt your child to think about the feelings and reactions of others.*

Ask your child to think about the needs of others. For instance, "How do you think Joey felt when Danny pushed him?" "Why do you think Mary didn't invite Jackie to her birthday party?" Make sure you react calmly to what your child tells you. Listen completely to your child's responses before you offer your opinion. Your child needs to feel that his perspective is valued, even if you don't see things exactly the same way.

Step Three	*Help your child develop a larger, more detailed vocabulary of feelings.*

I can't overestimate the value for children of understanding their own feelings and being able to express them in a clear, calm fashion. Children with healthy social behaviors tend to have a solid understanding of their own feelings, which helps them tune in to others' feelings. To help your child learn more about his feelings, start by teaching your child a "Feeling of the Week." Begin with simple ones, like *mad, sad, glad,* and move on to more challenging ones like *frustrated, disappointed,* and *confused.* (See the box below for a list of feelings to review with your child.) I find it helpful to post the Feeling of the Week in an obvious place, such as on a bulletin board or on the refrigerator. Use the word in sentences regularly throughout the week, and point it out to your child if he exhibits that feeling.

Feelings List

mad	sad	glad	happy
disappointed	angry	upset	confused
frustrated	satisfied	interested	loving
affectionate	stressed	bored	pleased
thoughtful	shocked	dreamy	guilty
scared	sick	silly	excited
embarrassed	shy	surprised	irritable
lonely	anxious	grouchy	brave
jealous	tired	proud	worried

Make sure you express your own feelings clearly and openly with your child. Children learn a great deal from watching and imitating you. Your expression of feelings gives them permission to explore their own. Don't be afraid to say to your child things like: "I love your father, but I do get really angry with him sometimes"; "I'm so frustrated with my boss at work when he watches over me like a hawk"; or "I'm so disappointed in myself that I didn't make that deadline."

Step Four	*Help your child tune in to body language and facial expressions.*

Learning this skill can be a lot of fun. Help your child understand the motivations and feelings of others by observing out loud what others' faces and bodies are telling him. Highlight for your child the clues people give us to tell us what they are feeling. For example, notice how red faces and loud voices show anger, or how wide open eyes and mouths show surprise. You might want to talk with your child about what the facial expressions would look like for each of the feelings listed on the previous page.

Step Five | *Help your child notice verbal cues.*

Kids who have trouble reading social signals often cannot differentiate among different tones of voice. They may overreact to a limit-setting voice by thinking it's angry, or they may underreact to a child telling them to stop because they don't pick up on the seriousness of the tone. This is a hard skill to teach. Both Lauren and Andy have difficulty with this—Andy by misinterpreting verbal cues, and Lauren by not recognizing them.

One of the most common problems kids experience in this area is not stopping when others ask them to stop. This is especially noticeable between siblings. Have you ever witnessed your older child trying to get your younger one to stop an annoying behavior? It's practically impossible! This is extremely frustrating for the older sibling. The same kind of thing happens frequently on the playground or at recess. The best way to curtail this behavior is to reward your child when he stops doing something he's been asked to stop. For instance, if your four-year-old stops poking his big brother right away when his big brother asks him to stop, tell him how happy you are that he stopped right away.

Step Six | *Encourage a sense of humor.*

It's common knowledge that laughing is a healing emotion. Think about how good you feel after a long, hearty laugh. It's the same for children. But it's often hard to maintain a sense of humor. Many things can cause stress in your child's life, such as academic and peer pressures. You can help your child see the funny side of life. Tell jokes at the dinner table. Take your kids to funny movies.

And most importantly, teach your child to laugh at himself by laughing at your own foibles. The next time you make a mistake, point it out and laugh at yourself out loud. Help your child to see that mistakes are a part of life; it's okay to make them, learn from them, and move on.

Children who have the most trouble with teasing and bullies tend to be like Andy—they take the actions of others more seriously than was intended. Help your child notice when actions are benign rather than malevolent. Even though this won't always be the case, it doesn't hurt to assume there was no evil intent before jumping to conclusions. A good forum for working on these issues is with siblings at home. The sibling relationship is a perfect one for understanding and practicing the skills in this book. Practice with your child laughing stuff off with a sibling, and I guarantee you'll see it transfer to relationships at school and in the neighborhood.

| Step Seven | *Teach your child to respond empathetically to others.* |

Even if a child doesn't clearly understand the nuances expressed by others, it's still important that he respond *as if* he understands. For instance, if Julie tells Ashley that she had a fight with her mom, and Julie doesn't really understand what they were fighting about, it's still important for Julie to act as if she understands by appearing to be listening, nodding her head, and having a caring facial expression. It often happens that acting as if you understand can actually lead to understanding. If you act as if you are confident, for instance, in time you may actually feel confident. If you act as if you are sympathetic to someone else's problem, in time you may actually feel sympathetic.

In this vein, teach your child to say short words that express empathy. For example, "Oh" (said in a disappointed tone). Help him to maintain a facial expression and body stance that appears caring. You may want to practice this in front of a mirror. Spend some time choosing words and expressions that demonstrate empathetic listening. Gradually begin teaching your child to ask follow-up questions that help open up others instead of close them down. A statement that might close someone down is, "That's no big deal. That happens to me all the time," or "Why are you so upset about that?" Questions designed to open up others to you are, "What's bothering you?" and "Do you want to talk about it?"

When you see your child acting as if he's empathizing, reward him with specific praise. "You know, Sean, I feel like you cared about what I just said because you looked at me and put your hand on my arm to show you care. Thanks."

You might even want to set up a chart at home or in school for your child to monitor himself. You or the teacher asks your child to rate himself with a smiley face for positive social behavior, a neutral face for okay social behavior, and a frowning face for negative social behavior. See if your rating matches your child's. If it does, reward your child with a sticker or points to be traded in for privileges later. It's more important at the beginning that your child's rating match yours so you know he is seeing himself accurately. Ultimately, you want both a match and consistently positive social behavior.

Step Eight	Encourage your child to be flexible to accommodate others' feelings.

Help your child to recognize and appreciate the feelings of others by encouraging polite behavior. Allow guests in your home to choose what they want to play. Remind your child of the importance of going with the flow. Ask your child to tell you what kinds of things his friends like to play and do.

Encourage your child to always include, rather than exclude, other kids. Discourage cliques. Especially during the middle elementary years, inclusion vs. exclusion becomes a big issue. Girls, in particular, establish insiders and outsiders, winners and losers. Help your child learn to be tolerant and accepting of others, and appreciate that the world is made up of all kinds of children with all kinds of interests.

Andy and Lauren Learn to Read Social Signals

Andy's parents did the right thing in the beginning by listening carefully to Andy's perceptions of what was happening to him at school. They neither judged him, dismissed him, nor overreacted to what he told them. Going to speak to his teacher was an excellent move because it gave his parents another perspective on what was happening at school. If Andy was being bullied or threatened, the school authorities would need to know so they could take appropriate action. If Andy wasn't being bullied, but instead was overreacting to others' actions, his parents would need to know so they could help their son.

After the conversation with Andy's teacher, his parents gave him extra support. His Dad told him about his own personal experiences with feeling picked on and how he handled it. Both of his parents began teasing him a bit in a playful manner in hopes that this would help him develop a thicker skin. They showed him how to laugh at himself. They were very pleased that Andy engaged in role-playing exercises with them. For example, they pretended to bump into him in the hallway and he practiced ways to brush it off. Andy began to recognize the signs that indicate when actions are intended or accidental. He learned that if a person says he's sorry after he bumps you, that he probably didn't mean to bump you. And he realized that sometimes he, too, bumped into people in a crowded hallway, and he didn't mean to do it either. Andy eventually befriended a boy who shared a few classes with him, and they spent time together at lunch and walking to class. This friendship helped Andy feel more secure at school. Pretty soon, Andy stopped complaining to his parents about being picked on. He appeared happier and more in control of his life.

While Andy had just one major issue to deal with, Lauren has several. She wants to be liked and to have friends, but she doesn't quite know how to get others to like her. Lauren's parents decided to embark upon a more formalized social skills training program to improve her skills. They could not afford to bring her to a private therapist or a group program, so they decided to train her themselves. They bought several books on social skills training. They enrolled her in a "lunch bunch" at her school with fellow classmates who offered support and feedback to each other while they learned social skills. They exposed Lauren to as many social activities as possible, signing her up for things like horseback riding and art class—activities that were cooperative, not competitive, in nature.

Her parents took a step-by-step approach to the problem. They chose a different skill each month to work on with Lauren. They informed her teacher what they were working on and asked her teacher to reinforce the skills Lauren exhibited at school. They spent a lot of time helping Lauren expand her expression and understanding of feelings. They read books to her and asked her how she thought the characters were feeling and what made them act the way they did. Lauren's progress was slow, but steady. After a year of intensive work focusing on social issues, Lauren's teacher reported that the teasing in the classroom had subsided. She said that Lauren's behavior was less disruptive, and that she was beginning to play with others at the playground. Lauren's parents were pleased with their daughter's progress and continued to teach Lauren the social skills necessary for her to make and keep friends.

Reading Social Signals Games and Exercises

1. Read books with your children.

Stop and discuss how the characters in the story might be feeling.

2. Look at magazine pictures showing facial expressions and body language.

Write captions to go with the expressions.

3. Draw a neutral face, a happy face, a sad face, a confused face, and so on.

Make comments about each face.

4. Name the Feeling Game

Watch TV or movies together. Pause and discuss what the characters might be feeling and how they are communicating their feelings.

5. The Mirror Game

Have your child stand in front of a mirror and express feelings. Ask your child to comment on whether the feelings were clearly expressed. You also can videotape your child and do the same exercise.

6. The Hat Trick Game

Put pieces of paper with different feelings written on them inside one hat. (Hat #1 will contain papers saying "happy," "sad," "scared," "frustrated," "excited," "angry," and so on.) Put pieces of paper with tasks written on them inside another hat. (Hat #2's papers will read "say hello to friend," "take off your coat," "ask a friend over to hang out," and so on.) Have your child choose one "feeling" and one "task" from each hat. The object of the game is to perform the tasks while conveying the feeling. Others must guess what the feelings are. The goal of the game is for children to increase their awareness of others' feelings and for the performer to express feelings more clearly.

7. The Charades Game

The goal of this game is to guess the feelings behind the body language. A family member strikes a pose and freezes. Everyone else must guess what the poser is feeling. You can increase the level of difficulty by making the feelings more challenging.

8. People Watch

Sit in a good people-watching spot with your child, perhaps on a park bench. Observe out loud together what you think people's facial expressions and body language are communicating. Try to make up stories about people based on their appearance. Ask questions like, "What do you think that man does for work?" or "Where do you think that person is going?" Notice the cues that let us understand how others feel. Then wonder aloud about their motivations. "Why do you think that child is crying?" "What does that mother's face say about what she is feeling?" Highlight for your child the clues people give us to tell us what they're feeling. "Notice that her face is red, her voice is loud, her jaw is clenched. That woman must be angry!" Play guessing games with your child to see if he can guess the feelings of others.

9. The School Chart

Set up a chart at home or in school for your child to monitor himself. You or the teacher asks your child to rate himself with a smiley face for good social skills, a neutral face for okay social skills, and a frowning face for negative social behavior. See if your rating and/or the teacher's matches your child's. If it does, reward your child with a sticker or points to be traded in for privileges later. It's more important at the beginning that your child's rating match yours and/or the teacher's so you know he is seeing himself accurately. Ultimately, you want both a match and good social skills.

10. Videotaping

Tape your child without him knowing. Sometimes children have no idea how they appear to others. Whenever we videotape the kids in our training group, most of them are amazed at what they see on tape. "I can't believe I did that!" This technique allows kids to see themselves through others' eyes and helps them alter their actions based on the reactions of others.

11. The Tape Recording Game

Tape yourself with a tape recorder saying the same word repeatedly, but use a different tone of voice each time you say it. Play it back for your child and see if he can differentiate what the feeling is behind each word. For instance, if you choose the word *stay*, first say it in an angry way, then in a firm but unemotional way, then as if you are asking a question, then as if you are frustrated, and so on. This exercise is harder than it seems. Give it a try!

Chapter Five

RAISING
SELF-ESTEEM

Putting It All Together

Managing Anger

Resolving Conflicts

Solving Social Problems

Managing Stress

Coping with Teasing

Raising Self-Esteem

Reading Social Signals

Communicating and Conversing

Joining In

Getting Started

GOALS ▸

In this chapter, you will learn how to help your child:

✓ Realistically evaluate his strengths and weaknesses.

✓ Appreciate the differences between himself and others.

✓ Use self-monitoring techniques.

✓ Use positive self-talk.

✓ Take responsibility for his actions.

✓ Accept mistakes and learn from them.

✓ Take credit for his accomplishments.

✓ Respect the needs of others.

Emily

E mily is a seven-year-old who gives up easily and doesn't seem to have confidence that she can solve the problems she encounters. Her parents describe her as a very bright underachiever. Her teachers say they overhear her calling herself stupid when she makes mistakes in class. Her perfectionism extends to her classmates—she is also very intolerant of any mistakes they make. She corrects them constantly and seems to need to be in charge of everything they do. Her classmates originally accepted Emily's behavior, but now they have become resentful of her. They are beginning to avoid contact with her, and she rarely receives invitations to play after school and on weekends.

Jack

Jack is a nine-year-old who on the surface appears to be quite confident. He is always sneaking into his conversations how smart he is. As a way of proving this, he'll engage in "one upmanship" battles with his friends. "I bet you don't know what 123×245 is." Whenever one of Jack's classmates tells him about something he is proud of, Jack always has to tell a bigger and better story. The kids in the neighborhood don't like to play with him because they say he "cheats" and "changes the rules" all of the time. Jack's mom has received a few phone calls from other parents telling her that Jack has been picking on some of the younger kids at the bus stop. He teases smaller kids and tries to challenge them to a fight. Jack's parents are very concerned about this behavior, especially because Jack used to be bullied a lot. Now he seems to be turning into a bully himself.

Both Jack and Emily suffer from low self-esteem. These children have adopted certain behaviors as compensating mechanisms for feeling poorly about themselves. As you can see from just the two examples above, there are different ways low self-esteem can be exhibited in a child.

✏ The Self-Esteem Quiz

Take the following quiz to see if your child may need a self-esteem boost:

☐ Is your child realistic about his strengths and limitations?

☐ Does your child carry himself with good posture?

☐ Can he laugh along when others playfully tease him?

☐ Does he accept constructive criticism and change his behavior accordingly?

☐ Does he accept your praise and continue the positive behavior?

☐ Is your child tolerant of others' differences? (Intolerance is evident when your child judges others harshly or teases others' weaknesses.)

☐ Is your child able to calm himself down easily when he's upset?

☐ Does your child take pride in his appearance by dressing neatly, cleanly, and appropriately?

☐ Is your child able to express his own needs to peers in an assertive voice?

☐ Does your child accept responsibility for his mistakes?

☐ Can your child persevere even when he is frustrated?

☐ Does your child cope effectively with frustration?

☐ Is your child able to say "no" to peers?

☐ Does your child approach new people with confidence?

☐ Does your child engage in a new activity anticipating success?

These questions address not only how your child feels about himself, but also whether he is able to accept responsibility for his actions. If you answered *yes* to all of these questions, then you can just skip over this chapter. If you answered *no* to some of them, it would be worthwhile for you to continue reading and try some of the exercises in this chapter.

What Does Self-Esteem Have To Do With Good Social Skills?

Much research has been published in recent years stressing the importance of high self-esteem to a child's emotional development. Check out your local bookstore and you'll find many books on this topic. You may already know that self-esteem is important, but you may not know how to help your child develop high self-esteem. This chapter focuses on how self-esteem affects the quality of your child's peer relationships and how you, as a parent, can help your child feel good about himself. Once your child has acquired high self-esteem, it will be much easier for him to establish the kind of friendships he needs. "You can't love others until you love yourself" is as true for friendship as it is for love. "You can't *have* a friend until you *are* a friend."

The children I work with give these definitions of self-esteem: "It's how we feel about ourselves"; "If you have self-esteem, you like yourself"; "I'm okay so I have it." When we think about self-esteem, we usually think about it in terms of thoughts and feelings about ourselves.

What we sometimes forget is that self-esteem also refers to feelings of competency and control.

Children with low self-esteem feel no empowerment; they feel that no matter what they do, they can't make a difference. If good things happen to children with low self-esteem, they believe it was a fluke. When bad things happen to them, they think it was bad luck or someone else's fault. For example, a child with low self-esteem might say, "I only caught that fly ball because it came right to me." A child with high self-esteem would say, "I caught that fly because I've been practicing a lot with my dad." A child with learning difficulties who has low self-esteem might say, "I flunked that test because the teacher hates me." The child with high self-esteem will take responsibility for his own actions and say, "I didn't study hard enough for that test. Next time I'm giving myself more time to prepare." A child with low self-esteem and difficulty making friends might say, "All the kids in class are mean to me because they are jerks!" A child with high self-esteem who has the same peer problems would say instead, "Gee, I wonder how I could change my behavior so that others will like me."

> Children with little self-assurance will make different social choices than children who believe in themselves.

Children with little self-assurance will make different social choices than children who believe in themselves. Those with low self-esteem tend to choose others with poor self-esteem. These choices have consequences, which can further lower self-esteem. And so the cycle continues.

Self-Esteem Affects Emily's and Jack's Peer Relations

Emily feels as though the mistakes she makes are a reflection of who she is. She calls herself "stupid." In trying to gain control over her life she makes poor social choices—for example, by telling others what to do. This behavior causes others to avoid her. Emily doesn't understand her peers' reactions and feels hurt. Her self-esteem is further diminished.

Jack is stuck in a similar cycle. He overcompensates for feeling badly about himself by boasting. Bragging and putting others down gives him a feeling of power that he doesn't know how to acquire any other way. These behaviors result in poor peer relationships, which further damages his self-esteem. To compensate, Jack defends himself by setting himself further apart from his classmates. And so the cycle continues.

In both Jack and Emily's situations, we cannot separate how they feel about themselves from how they treat their peers. Children with a positive, solid sense of self-worth are able to take into account the needs of others. Treating others with respect is a visible reflection of a child's high self-esteem. Here is a list of behaviors we generally associate with high and low self-esteem:

Kids With High Self-Esteem:	Kids With Low Self-Esteem:
▸ Have a relaxed and balanced posture	▸ Often blame others for their own actions
▸ Maintain good eye contact with others	▸ Might speak too loudly or too softly
▸ Have alert and bright eyes	▸ Need to be liked by everyone
▸ Socialize well with others	▸ See themselves as losers
▸ Have good personal hygiene	▸ Are critical of others
▸ Have friends with high self-esteem	▸ Have trouble making and keeping friends
▸ Are realistically aware of their own strengths and limitations	▸ Have difficulty accepting compliments
▸ Can accept rejection or critical feedback	▸ Have trouble accepting responsibility for their actions
▸ Can say "no" to peers	▸ Get frustrated easily
▸ Set small goals and achieve them	▸ Make negative comments about themselves
▸ Are able to tune into other people's needs	▸ Tend to be quitters
▸ Have "stick-to-it-ness"	▸ May brag
▸ Have fairly stable moods	▸ Can be bullies

"Did I Create Low Self-Esteem In My Child?"

Being a parent is an enormous responsibility and we often wonder if we're doing a good job at it. Often I have heard parents say, "I dearly love my child, I'm always encouraging her and praising her, and yet she is still so hard on herself," or "Why does my child have such low self-esteem? What have I done to him?" or "When I tell my child she's terrific, she doesn't believe me. What can I do?"

It continues to surprise me that many children who grow up in comfortable, loving, safe homes can still suffer from low self-esteem. And likewise, there are children I know who have endured unspeakable abuses, unstable family situations, and terribly unsafe living conditions, and still manage to hold on to a solid sense of self-worth. As a young therapist, before I had my own children, I found it easy to hold parents responsible for their child's social and emotional makeup. "If these parents only did 'thus-and-such,' their child would be so much better off." "Why can't they just blah, blah, blah," I'd think. Perhaps that attitude helped me feel more in control back then.

> A child comes into this world with a unique temperament, part of which is inherited.

But now I know that a child comes into this world with a unique temperament, part of which is inherited. Some babies are peaceful and placid right from birth, while others are not. There are babies who are slow to warm up to people, and babies who are hypersensitive to external stimulation. There are criers and there are whiners. There are those who are eager to engage with others and those who are more cautious.

A baby with a complex temperament may be more prone to self-esteem issues. His reactions are more unpredictable. For instance, a smile from a parent may not necessarily result in a smile from the baby. As a result of his temperament, a difficult child will more likely be treated differently than will an easy child who fits in more naturally. After all, a difficult child can make a caretaker feel very inadequate. Parents frequently find that successful methods used to raise their first child do not work at all with their more complicated second child. This doesn't mean, however, that this child's life is set in stone. This is where the child's environment comes in.

> A baby with a complex temperament may be more prone to self-esteem issues.

Throughout their lives, children are affected by many important outside influences. Teachers, siblings, grandparents, and friends all impact your child's self-esteem. Your child's natural disposition will make it either easier or harder for others to appreciate him. For instance, a child who misbehaves in the classroom is most likely going to get negative feedback from his teacher. This, in turn, perpetuates bad feelings, continuing the cycle of negative interaction.

As a parent, you cannot completely control who interacts with your child, but you can make sure that you create an atmosphere at home and in your family life where your child can flourish. It's important that you first accept your child's unique qualities and let go of unrealistic expectations of him. This doesn't mean that you stop setting appropriate limits and boundaries. You need to become aware of any personal feelings of disappointment you may have about your child, and then work to not let those feelings dominate your interactions with him. Focus instead on your child's strengths and competencies. We need to accept who our child is, and then learn how to create an environment in which he can flourish.

Raising Your Child's Self-Esteem

The following steps will help you create a safe and nurturing environment in which your child can develop high self-esteem. Please keep in mind your child's unique temperament when practicing these techniques.

| Step One | *Encourage areas of competence.* |

Help your child find "areas of competence" as stepping stones on the road toward high self-esteem. Support your child in finding his strengths (sports, computers, music, drama, and so on) and encourage his involvement in these activities. If your child struggles in areas that society highly values, such as school or playing team sports, he may feel tremendous self-doubt. Children need to experience a sense of accomplishment to feel good about themselves. It's up to you to help your child discover his areas of competence and reinforce those strengths.

It sometimes can be difficult for parents when their children have interests that are very different from their own. For example, I once worked with a man named John who was a former professional football player. John's son, Tony, was quite uncoordinated and hated sports. John tried to get his son to play sports with him, but Tony resisted. Instead, Tony spent his free time collecting things —stamps, action figures, beanie babies. Tony often asked his father to help him with his collections, but John wasn't interested and brushed him off. "Maybe later, son." It took John some time to deal with his own feelings of disappointment in not having a sports-playing son. Once he did, however, he recognized how he hurt Tony by not supporting his interests. John began to help Tony with his collecting. This not only helped improved Tony's self-esteem, but it also brought father and son closer.

I'm often asked the question, "What if my son wants to play the same thing all the time? Should I still encourage it?" Yes, but within limits. As an example, let's say you have a child who plays on the computer a lot. I have seen children playing computer games nonstop, often for hours on end. They obviously feel safe and confident in that arena. In this case, I would recommend that you limit the amount of time on the computer and encourage your child to challenge himself in different ways. Perhaps he could use his talents to help other children and become a computer tutor.

| Step Two | *Promote physical fitness.* |

Regardless of your child's particular areas of competence, physical activity must be a part of your child's normal routine. If your child is opposed to playing team sports, that's okay. How about horseback riding? Or martial arts? Or bike riding? American children are more obese now than ever, and a major reason for this is an increase in sedentary activities, such as playing video and computer games and watching television. Do not give your child a choice about this issue. He may choose what *kind* of activity he wants to participate in, but not *whether* an activity is necessary.

In addition, make sure your child eats a nutritionally balanced diet. A balanced diet and regular exercise not only will give your child energy, it will also improve his appearance. All of this adds up to high self-esteem.

| Step Three | *Encourage your child constantly.* |

It may seem obvious that parents need to encourage their children if high self-esteem is to develop. But often in our hectic lives we tend to focus solely on discipline, rather than on guidance and encouragement. We tend not to pay much attention when behavior is positive, but we exert a lot of energy when we see behavior that needs correcting. Here's an idea: try doing the reverse!

1. Spend more time attending to positive behavior than to negative.

Make your disciplinary statements short and sweet, without harshness. Say many more things that praise your child. You can even turn your disciplinary statements into praise statements. For instance, a negative correction might be, "No more TV. It's homework time." A praise statement might be, "I like it when you start your homework as soon as I ask you to. It makes me feel good to see you take such responsibility for your schoolwork."

2. Engage in small and easy ways to encourage self-esteem during the course of a day.

Anytime you see your child do something well, let him know. Write caring notes to your child and sneak them into a lunch box or leave them out on a bedroom pillow. Spend fifteen minutes a day of "special time" with your child. Let him decide how to spend that time with you. Go with his flow and enjoy!

3. Encourage your child's independence.

Listen carefully when he tells you about his problems. Avoid answering questions too quickly. Let your child struggle a little to find his own solutions. Allow your child to make choices. "Which shoes do you want to wear?" "Who do you want to play with this afternoon?" "Do you want green beans or broccoli for a vegetable tonight?" Allow your child to do things for himself. Assume that he can complete tasks without your help, and most of the time he will surprise you. Perhaps you dress your four-year-old each day, assuming he can't dress himself. If you allow him to dress himself and praise him for doing so, he will feel more confident. (Be careful not to criticize his clothing choices.)

Step Four	*Praise and discipline your child, choosing your words carefully.*

Your words are very important to your child. The way you offer praise and deliver criticism can help your child develop high self-esteem. Try the following techniques:

Praise

1. **Be specific with your praise.**

2. **Praise your child immediately following a positive action.**

3. **Make sure you praise genuinely.**

Children will detect it if you're being insincere. Children do need to know that not everything they do is wonderful. Sometimes a "you can do better" helps them to strive toward a goal.

4. **Praise "steps in the right direction" rather than "the end result."**

For instance, rather than waiting until a homework assignment is finished before you praise your child, praise him for spending lots of time on one assignment or comment on how well he concentrates.

Discipline

1. **Use positives rather than negatives.**

Criticize constructively. Avoid words like "don't." Instead, focus on the good behavior you want to encourage. For instance, instead of saying, "Don't put your shoes on the kitchen table," try saying, "I'd like to see your shoes in the closet where they belong." Or even point to the shoes and then to the closet, saying, "Shoes. Closet." These words let your child know what's expected of him without putting him down. This technique seems simple, but actually is quite difficult to do. "Don't" words tend to come much more easily than "Do" ones.

2. Avoid using labels like "always" and "never."

Children feel trapped by these labels. Instead of saying, "You are always losing things!" say "You brought your coat home from school yesterday. I like when you remember your things."

3. Accept your child's feelings.

No parent likes to see a child feeling hurt, but in an effort to stop your child from crying or being angry, you may discount his emotions, saying things like, "That's nothing to cry about," "You're acting like a baby," or "Get over it!" Such comments leave your child feeling misunderstood and embarrassed by his emotions. Try instead to acknowledge his feelings. For instance, if your child is upset because he has to go to the dentist and he'd rather play with his friends, say, "I know you are disappointed, but it's important to take care of your teeth. We'll be leaving in five minutes." He still has to go to the dentist, but you have empathized with him first.

4. Set clear limits.

▶ Make sure when you give your child a direction that you mean it.

▶ Say the command clearly and firmly.

▶ Don't turn the direction into a question: "Would

you like to clean up your room?" (Your child will say "No!")

▸ Avoid the word "let's." "Let's clean up your room." This implies that you're going to help him clean.

▸ Before you give a command, make sure you have your child's attention—turn off the TV or computer.

Look into his eyes.

Give the command.

Wait silently for compliance (at least 30 seconds).

Impose an immediate consequence if the command is not followed. For instance, "Go upstairs and brush your teeth before bed." If the direction is not followed, say, "You have not done what I have asked. For each minute I wait for you to go upstairs, you have to go to bed that many minutes earlier."

▸ Instead of nagging, set clear limits. The problem with nagging is that it's not just annoying to your child, it also leaves you very frustrated. The chances of you blowing your top after a bout of nagging are pretty high. And yelling at your child is not good for your child's self-esteem.

Look at the following self-esteem "boosters" and "busters." How often do you say these things?

| Step Five | *Encourage positive self-talk.* |

Perhaps you have heard your child say things like, "I stink at this," "I can't do this," or "I hate myself." These words perpetuate feelings of hopelessness. When your child is experiencing an emotional situation, the thoughts that go through his head can be either helpful by urging him forward, or hurtful by holding him back. A child who says negative things to himself is not going to soothe himself; rather, his words will stir him to new heights of anger. Give your child new language to soothe himself in difficult times. "I'm mad but I can get through this." "I'm in control of myself." You've heard the expression, "mind over matter." It's important to encourage your child to stay focused and positive so that he can accomplish his goals. Listen to your child's negative self-statements and then respond positively. Try some of these, and come up with some of your own.

- ▸ "Nobody is good at everything."
- ▸ "I'll get better if I keep trying."
- ▸ "I'll do better when I'm not so tired or frustrated."
- ▸ "Maybe I'm not such a great speller, but I have lots of good ideas to write down."
- ▸ "I can do this."
- ▸ "When I put my mind to it, I can accomplish almost anything."

Step Six	*Provide opportunities for self-monitoring.*

A basic component of high self-esteem is the ability to observe ourselves and to change our behavior to fit the demands of a particular situation. To encourage this ability, you can provide opportunities for your child to observe his own behavior and then make decisions about how to proceed. Children rebel against rules when they don't understand them or when they are imposed unpredictably.

If children are made aware of behavioral guidelines in advance of situations, they feel more a part of the decision-making process. They know in advance what the expectations are. This encourages them to take responsibility for their own actions, which is a key element of high self-esteem.

> Children rebel against rules when they don't understand them or when they are imposed unpredictably.

For example, try this for a child who has behavioral problems in the classroom. Give him a piece of paper with two columns—one for the morning and one for the afternoon. Ask him to monitor his own behavior throughout the day. If he behaves appropriately, he draws in a happy face. If he misbehaves, he draws in a sad face. The goal of this exercise is for the child's observations to match his teacher's, since the teacher is also drawing the faces on a separate paper. If the child matches the teacher, he is rewarded. This gives the child a sense of control over his behavior. Even if they both draw sad faces, the child is rewarded for an accurate assessment. He is given a better reward for matching two happy faces. He is not rewarded at all if he doesn't match. This kind of exercise teaches a child to observe his behavior accurately and then to change it, if necessary.

Step Seven | *Encourage socialization.*

As children develop, healthy peer relationships begin to have a greater impact on how they see themselves. In the elementary years, it's no longer enough just to have parental love. The respect and acceptance of friends is almost as important. For this reason, you must develop your child's social networks early. Start by setting up play dates and play groups during the toddler years, and then continue to encourage peer relationships straight through elementary school.

1. Help your child appreciate and accept differences between himself and others.

Remember that your child will directly pick up from you your level of tolerance and willingness to include others. Be careful what you say in front of your child. This may seem obvious, but if you have strong negative feelings toward another person or group of people, your child will tend to pick up on that and mirror your sentiments.

2. Study other children.

Notice their clothing and how they wear their hair. Your child does not need to be a carbon copy of your next door neighbor, but it's important that you not set up your child to be teased, either. Highly unusual dress and hairstyles can make your child a target for teasing. (In adolescence, the issues change. Your child may actively seek to look "different.")

3. Set clear rules for hygiene.

Make sure your child bathes regularly, brushes his teeth at least twice every day, and wears clean clothes. These behaviors may need to be reinforced with positive rewards (see page eleven for reward ideas).

4. Be careful with sibling relationships.

Although they can be a great avenue for learning social lessons, they also can be prime ground for hurtful comparisons. Don't compare siblings, even if your children want to. If your children are fighting with each other, try to not get involved unless there is physical aggression. Listen to what they have to say, validate their feelings, check to make sure they are not hurt, and then move on.

5. Encourage your child to socialize with other children who have high self-esteem.

Make sure your child is involved in extracurricular activities, especially during adolescence. Encourage your child to befriend children with similar interests. We often worry that when our children become adolescents that they will fall in with "the wrong crowd." We fear our kids will succumb to peer pressure and get involved in destructive behaviors such as drugs, alcohol, and premature sexual activity. In my experience, children with high self-esteem tend to engage in healthy peer relationships. Their self-confidence gives them the ability to evaluate situations objectively and to make appropriate judgments about them.

Step Eight	**Help your child learn from mistakes.**

Children with low self-esteem are terribly afraid of making mistakes. And this fear makes it very difficult for them to take chances. It also can make it hard for them to follow through with activities. Instead, they become quitters because they're afraid they won't perform the activity perfectly. You can help your child get over the fear of failure, although it's not an easy task. Try the following:

1. Bring attention to your own mistakes.

React calmly when you make mistakes. Allow your child to see how you handle errors. Speak out loud about the mistakes you make and how you learn from them.

2. React calmly to your child's mistakes.

Don't say demeaning things like, "I told you it wouldn't work," "That was not a smart thing to do," or "You weren't thinking straight." Instead, say out loud, "I bet we can learn something from this," or "Don't worry. Everyone makes mistakes."

3. Always focus on what children do well rather than on what they don't do well.

For instance, if your child has sloppy handwriting, instead of pointing that out in general, you might comment on how neatly he wrote one particular word.

4. Talk about your own childhood blunders.

Discuss how you lived through them and what you learned from them.

Regardless of how high your child's self-esteem is, the above strategies can significantly increase his feelings of competence. A beneficial side effect of changing your own communication skills is that your relationship with your child improves and you both feel energized by the experience.

Self-Esteem Tips for Kids

☐ Set small goals and try to meet them.

☐ Hang around positive people who seem to like you for who you are.

☐ Learn how to accept constructive criticism and put it to good use.

☐ Say "thank you" to a compliment and let yourself feel good about receiving it.

☐ Compliment others.

☐ Learn to speak to others as you would like them to speak to you.

☐ Express yourself with words, not actions, when your feelings are hurt.

☐ Learn to laugh at yourself.

☐ Walk with confidence—head high, good eye contact, good posture.

☐ Pay attention to the things you're good at and don't worry about the things that are hard for you.

☐ Bathe and brush your teeth regularly and wear clean clothes. When you look your best, you'll feel your best.

Self-Esteem Games and Exercises

1. Thinking Straight and Feeling Great!

This exercise is designed to help your child see a potentially negative situation in a new light. Have your child choose a situation that makes him feel badly about himself. Try to help him change negative thoughts to positive ones by talking through a situation with your child:

Positive Self-Talk Worksheet

What am I thinking about this situation?

_____

_____

_____

Which thoughts are negative thoughts?

_____

_____

_____

What are some positive thoughts about the situation?

_____

_____

_____

What is my new way of feeling about this situation?

_____

_____

_____

2. Family Fun

Place a jar of checkers or marbles in the middle of your table during a family dinner. Ask each family member to make a positive statement about himself. Every positive statement is rewarded with a checker. The winner is the one with the most checkers at the end.

3. Fill in the Blanks

Ask your child to write down the answers to these questions.
I am proud of:

_____

_____

Things that I would like to change about myself are:

_____

_____

4. Accomplishment Scavenger Hunt

Hold an accomplishment scavenger hunt. During a family gathering or a party with friends, hand out the following list to everyone. Each participant must go around the room and write down others' names next to the accomplishments he made.

☐ Has been nice to a friend
☐ Was a member of a team sport
☐ Did my homework regularly
☐ Faced a fear alone
☐ Took care of a pet
☐ Told someone how I feel

☐ Won a prize or award
☐ Made a mistake and learned from it
☐ Was helpful to my brother or sister
☐ Tried a new activity even though it was hard for me

5. List of Strengths

Begin to make a list of your child's strengths. Leave the list out in a visible place, and add to it daily as you witness your child's positive attributes. Here are some examples (a–z) you might include on your list:

a. assertive	b. brave	c. cooperative
d. daring	e. energetic	f. funny
g. gentle	h. helpful	i. independent
j. jovial	k. kind	l. loving
m. musical	n. neat	o. original
p. peaceful	q. quiet	r. respectful
s. strong	t. trusting	u. unique
v. vivacious	w. willful	x. Xtra special
y. yielding	z. zestful	

6. Thought Stop

Develop a signal with your child to help him stop negative thoughts. For instance, your child could choose the code word "Shazam." Whenever he says something negative about himself, say "Shazam" to signal him to change his thoughts.

7. I Think I Can

Make "I think I can" bumper stickers. Post them all over your house to help your family remain positive. Here are some suggested phrases:

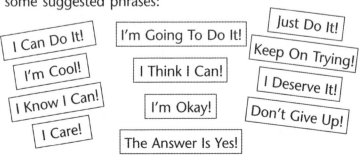

I Can Do It!

I'm Going To Do It!

Just Do It!

I'm Cool!

Keep On Trying!

I Think I Can!

I Know I Can!

I Deserve It!

I'm Okay!

I Care!

Don't Give Up!

The Answer Is Yes!

Chapter Six

COPING WITH TEASING

Putting It All Together

Managing Anger

Resolving Conflicts

Solving Social Problems

Managing Stress

Coping with Teasing

Raising Self-Esteem

Reading Social Signals

Communicating and Conversing

Joining In

Getting Started

GOALS ▸

In this chapter, you will learn how to help your child:

- ✔ Differentiate between different types of teasing.
- ✔ Control behavior that provokes teasing.
- ✔ Develop strategies to cope with teasing.
- ✔ Identify and avoid bullies.
- ✔ Know when to involve an adult.

Chris

*L*ately, Chris wants to stay home from school more and more. In second grade, he enjoyed going to school, but now that he is in third grade, he dreads going. Almost every day he complains of having a stomachache. Mom took him to the pediatrician, but the doctor could find nothing wrong. Chris has always been a rather timid, unassertive boy who normally plays with only one child at a time, but now he never brings anyone home to play. Mom is worried and asks him if anything at school is bothering him. At first, he says everything is fine. Then one day, Mom asks again and Chris starts to cry. Out pours a torrent of words. "The kids pick on me at school. Jimmy is a big bully. He says I'm stupid and pushes my books off my desk when the teacher isn't looking. The other kids are afraid of him and won't help me. When I tell the teacher, she tells me that I'm a big enough boy to fight my own battles. I don't want to go back to school. Ever!" When Mom asks about the other kids in class or what Chris does when Jimmy is mean to him, Chris says, "I try to ignore him, but he just keeps being* mean to me." When Mom tells Chris's dad about the situation, Dad wants to find Jimmy and "handle it" for Chris. "Nobody is going to pick on my son like that!" Mom doesn't want to talk to Jimmy. She is furious at the school for allowing this situation to continue. She wants to call the principal and demand a change of classroom for Chris.

Katherine

*K*atherine is a nine-year-old girl who continuously provokes others around her. She talks nonstop in class, preventing others from getting their work done. Her desk is such a mess that her stuff always ends up on other classmates' desks. She blurts out answers in class, which frustrates the teacher. The boys chase her at recess when she taunts them. Katherine doesn't understand why the other girls in class won't talk to her. They constantly whisper about Katherine behind her back and tell other girls not to play with her. Katherine never gets chosen for teams in gym class. The girls complain when the gym teacher assigns Katherine to their team. Katherine often gets hate notes left on her desk. Sometimes she tries to ignore the other girls. But often she just can't help crying when they're mean to her.

Teasing is one of the most painful experiences of childhood. Whether a child is being teased or doing the teasing, either way he will suffer greatly in his ability to sustain friendships and other peer relationships.

The Teasing Quiz

Take the following quiz to see if your child is being teased or is teasing others:

☐ Does your child present himself to others as shy, anxious, or insecure?

☐ Is your child restless, immature, and provocative to others?

☐ Does your child seem pleased or amused when others are picked on?

☐ Does your child frequently interpret teasing as hostile even when the teasing appears good-natured?

☐ Does your child provoke teasing by teasing others first?

☐ Does your child tend to overreact to teasing by crying or becoming enraged and lashing back physically?

☐ Does your child tell you he gets teased a lot?

☐ Does your child's teacher say your child bullies others?

☐ Does your child's teacher say others tease your child?

☐ Does your child complain of not knowing how to handle being teased by others?

If you answered *no* to all of these questions, then you can just skip over this chapter. If you answered *yes* to some of them, it would be worthwhile for you to continue reading this chapter.

Do Girls and Boys Tease the Same?

Girls and boys are equally likely to be teased. But the way boys and girls tease is quite different. As in Katherine's case, girls who are teased often become socially ostracized. Rather than launch a head-on assault like boys do, girls tend to tease indirectly. A female ringleader will whisper behind your daughter's back rather than call her names or physically confront her. The ringleader will make sure that no one invites your daughter to parties. Your child may find mean notes in her desk and hear false gossip being spread about her. Girls make it very clear who is "in" and who is "out." Because of the "back-door" nature of female teasing, it can be complicated to reckon with.

Boys, on the other hand, tend to be more straightforward in their teasing. They use more blunt methods—name calling, mimicking, and physical threatening. Your son may complain of being pushed, tripped on the lunch line, shoved into a locker, or having his books thrown on the ground.

Whether being teased by a girl or a boy, it can be very painful. The worst teasing from girls typically happens in grades three through six. By the time kids go to middle school, most of the teasing seems to come from the boys. In high school, the teasing seems to dissipate for both sexes. It's during high school that social alienation can become a serious issue for those kids who did not build successful friendships when they were younger.

Because teasing behavior tends to occur throughout the elementary school years, it's important to identify it early. Once you know if your child is being teased or is teasing others, you can take the steps recommended in this chapter to turn things around.

Do I Have a "Teaser" or a "Teasee"?

A "teasee" is a kid who gets teased by a "teaser." I've seen two different types of teasees—"The Worrier" and "The Provocateur."

The Worrier

The Worrier appears anxious, insecure, and lacking in self-confidence. Chris is an example of a Worrier. He tries to ignore the teasing and often is successful at it. But when it gets overwhelming, he breaks down in tears or in a flare of temper. He doesn't understand humorous teasing, and would never think of teasing another child, even in good fun. The Worrier gets targeted for teasing because he appears weak and emotionally vulnerable, which fuels the teaser's desire for power.

Signs of a Worrier

☐ Seems insecure

☐ Takes teasing too seriously

☐ Cries easily

☐ Is physically weak

☐ Has somatic complaints like bellyaches and headaches

The Provocateur

On the other hand, we have the Provocateur. The Provocateur is victimized because he unwittingly annoys other children. He is restless, cranky, and unable to read social signals appropriately. He doesn't stop when other kids tell him to stop and, in an attempt to fit in, will tease others first. Katherine fits this description. The Provocateur may fight back when teased, but will usually lose the fight. He cannot distinguish between good-natured teasing and mean teasing, and is liable to overreact to teasing, which further aggravates the situation.

Signs of a Provocateur

☐ Acts restless and fidgety

☐ Misreads social signals often

☐ Teases other kids first

☐ Can dish it out, but can't take it

☐ Doesn't stop when others tell him to stop

☐ Speaks loudly and talks too much

☐ Invades other kids' body space

It's important to notice any changes in your child's behavior. Sometimes when children are being picked on, they are too embarrassed to tell an adult about it. This is what happened with Chris. Initially, he was reluctant to tell his mom he was being teased. The following are some of the signs to look for which may indicate your child is being teased:

Signs Your Child May Be Getting Teased

- ☐ A drop in school grades
- ☐ A reluctance to go to school
- ☐ An increase in somatic complaints like headaches and stomachaches
- ☐ Missing lunch money and other personal items
- ☐ An increase in emotional outbursts at home
- ☐ Unexplained injuries
- ☐ A decrease in social activity after school and on weekends

The Teaser

The teaser tends to be a child who likes to dominate others. He may have a lot of friends that follow his orders. As long as the teaser does not become physically aggressive, but instead controls others with words only, he may maintain a group of followers throughout his school years. Physically aggressive bullies often lose their friends in elementary school because children are afraid of them and do not admire their behavior. But if the teaser's behavior is mainly verbal aggression and intimidation, he can usually hang on to his friends.

Signs of a Teaser

☐ Likes to be in control of social situations

☐ Lacks empathy for kids who get teased

☐ Appears cocky, self-confident, and arrogant

☐ Is very good at interacting with adults and saying what is expected

☐ Denies ever being teased

☐ Teases and bullies his siblings

☐ Has difficulty controlling his anger

Not All Teasing is the Same

Most of the teasing your child will experience is benign. Particularly with boys, teasing is just verbal sparring—it's a form of competition. Children who have a high social IQ understand this and do not take most teasing seriously. They know to laugh it off. They can easily distinguish harmless teasing from malicious teasing. But for the socially challenged child, teasing has a greater impact. For children who have been bullied, even good-natured teasing is threatening. If your child overreacts to benign teasing by crying, whining, throwing temper tantrums, shouting, or being physically aggressive, he will make things worse for himself. The first step is to help your child understand that most teasing is benign and good-natured.

When your child takes teasing lightly, chances are the teasers will move on to someone who takes them more seriously.

Types of Teasing

Help your child distinguish between the different types of teasing. This will lessen the impact of the teasing. Review the following list with your child and discuss what kinds of responses are required by different kinds of teasing.

- ▸ Name calling—"Fatty," "Four Eyes," "Geek"
- ▸ Putdowns—"You stink in math."
- ▸ Poking fun—"You are so silly sometimes."
- ▸ One-upmanship—"You're so slow. I could beat you walking."
- ▸ Mimicking—Repeating words in a sing-song voice.
- ▸ Whispering—Hand cupped over the mouth.
- ▸ Making you look foolish—Not responding to the "high five" sign.
- ▸ Practical jokes—A tack on your chair.
- ▸ Provoking—Continuing obnoxious behavior once someone has asked you to stop.
- ▸ Embarrassing—"You love Joey and want to kiss him!"
- ▸ Ganging up—All the kids laugh at the teasing.
- ▸ Bullying—Physical or emotional threatening.
- ▸ Destructive rumors—"I told everyone she stinks because she never takes a shower."
- ▸ Sarcasm—"Wow! Nice dress!" Tone conveys disdain.

Teasing Prevention

Your child's behavior could be contributing to his getting teased. Your child can control many of the behaviors that may result in teasing. Differentiate for your child the behaviors that he can control from those he can't. For instance, if a child gets teased because he has red hair, he can't change that. If he gets teased because he has poor hygiene, he can do something about that. Review the following checklist of teasing Do's and Don'ts and positively reinforce the good behaviors your child performs.

Do's:	Don'ts:
▸ Tease only when you and the teasee know that it's really just for fun.	▸ Don't tattle on others.
▸ Be aware of how others react. Sometimes a person's body language will tell you it's time to stop long before their words will.	▸ Don't get involved in somebody else's business.
	▸ Don't overreact.
	▸ Don't tease others.
▸ Know when it's time to stop. Not everybody can handle teasing.	▸ Don't provoke others (with a silly voice, mocking behavior, or disruptive noises).
▸ React calmly when teased. Try not to overreact or cry in front of others.	▸ Don't be a "goody-goody" (trying to control others' behavior in class).
▸ Look others straight in the eye and tell them how you feel.	▸ Don't talk too much.
	▸ Don't interrupt a lot.

(Do's and Don'ts continued on next page)

Do's:	Don'ts:
▶ Treat yourself with respect and others will respect you.	▶ Don't brag.
▶ Maintain good posture and carry your body with confidence so that people see that you respect yourself.	▶ Don't look scared a lot.
	▶ Don't stand with poor posture.
	▶ Don't use a timid voice.
▶ Use a calm, gentle tone of voice when talking and others will do the same.	▶ Don't have poor hygiene.
▶ Be a good listener. A good friend knows when to stop talking and listen.	▶ Don't display bad habits (for example, pick your nose or bite your fingernails).
▶ Go with the flow of the situation.	
▶ "MYOB" (mind your own business). If someone is not behaving well, let an adult take control.	
▶ Have a sense of humor about yourself.	
▶ Whenever possible, play with kids who you know like you.	

Preventing Teasing with Chris and Katherine

If we look again at the stories of Chris and Katherine, we can see how the teasing Do's and Don'ts might have prevented some of the teasing from happening. Katherine needs to work on controlling her behaviors that irritate others. She must become more aware of how her actions affect others. She needs to stop when others ask her to stop, go with the flow of the girls in her class, and stop provoking her classmates. Chris, on the other hand, must work on carrying himself with more authority, improving his posture, speaking in a more assertive tone of voice, and keeping his emotions in check. By teaching children to be proactive rather than reactive, we better their chances of not getting teased in the first place, or at least we can reduce their chances of continued teasing.

Teasing Survival Reminders

Remind your child that positive thoughts create positive actions. The Teasing Survival Reminders are positive comments your child can say to himself when he is in the midst of a difficult teasing situation. Ask your child to choose the statement or statements that *feel right for him.* Ask him to practice saying the sentences to himself when he is being teased. Check back with him regularly to see if he used his reminder and whether it helped him feel strong.

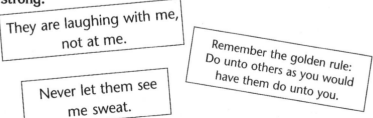

They are laughing with me, not at me.

Remember the golden rule: Do unto others as you would have them do unto you.

Never let them see me sweat.

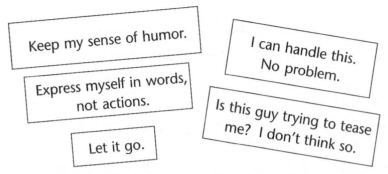

Your child may want to come up with his own reminders. Encourage him to use whatever works for him.

Talking With Your Child About Teasing

Children are often hesitant to talk to their parents about teasing. It's a difficult subject to discuss, and your child may be afraid you will judge him or tell him to just ignore the teasing. Approach the subject of teasing very carefully.

Step One	*Choose a time to talk when it's quiet and there are few distractions.*

Perhaps you can talk on a long car ride, at a dinner alone without siblings, or before bed.

Step Two	*Use a calm, casual, sympathetic tone of voice.*

Step Three	*Make an observation and wait patiently for the response.*

For example, "You seem like you had a hard day at school. Is something bothering you?"

Step Four | *If your child doesn't respond right away or denies that anything is bothering him, let him know that you are available to listen when he's ready.*

"Let me know if you feel like talking."

Step Five | *Show him you are listening by reflecting back what you hear him say.*

Review how to do this in Chapter Three on communicating and conversing.

Step Six | *Remain neutral.*

Do not criticize or act upset. Listen to the entire story. Then ask your child how you can be most helpful to him. It's important to listen to your child and get the whole picture before jumping in with a solution.

Step Seven | *If you're concerned that you're either not getting the whole story or you're getting a distorted picture, you may need to contact your child's teacher.*

Teachers generally have a very good idea of what's happening socially in the classroom. Other useful adults to contact are the gym teacher, the lunchroom monitor, and the recess monitor. These adults may know even more than the teacher because they see your child during less structured times of the day. If none of the school personnel has noticed anything, you can ask them to keep an eye on your child and report back to you with any new information.

Coping Effectively With Teasing

It's tempting to deal with teasing by fighting your child's battle for him. Teasing can be so painful for your child that you want to do anything to stop it. The problem with your stepping in is that first, it doesn't solve the problem, and second, it doesn't teach your child how to handle future teasing. And there is *always* future teasing. Many of the skills for dealing with teasing can be taught and practiced at home. You can role-play situations in which one person plays the teaser and the other plays the teasee. Practice the techniques below. Keep in mind that your child is going to need a variety of techniques because any one technique, if used too often, will become ineffective. You have to mix and match as the situation demands.

1. Laugh it off.

Teach your child to see the humor in teasing. Turn the tables on the teaser and make that child feel silly for teasing. This doesn't mean your child should tease back, which tends to make the teaser mad. The goal is to take away the power from the teaser by viewing the teasing as silly. Your child can show the teaser that the teasing isn't upsetting him. Some responses might be:

▸ "That's an old one."

▸ "You think I haven't heard that one before?"

▸ "Is that all you could come up with?"

▸ "Whoa. You're scaring me." (said sarcastically)

▸ "Your point is?"

▸ "Tell me something I haven't heard before."

2. Walk away.

Children often forget to walk away after they've responded to a teaser. They wait around for an answer. This continues the interaction instead of cutting it off immediately. Remind your child that he must walk away after he makes his retort. That way he is in control of the communication.

3. Learn systematic ignoring.

This is not the same as just plain ignoring someone. Systematic ignoring requires involvement in another activity. For example, if your child is being teased in the classroom and can't get away, he can pick up a pencil and paper and begin to write. While he is engaged in this other activity, he is thinking his survival reminder: "Keep my sense of humor."

4. Ask a distracting question.

This is a technique that can't be used too often, but it's very disarming when used once in a while. Eleven-year-old Sarah used this method when a group of boys were heckling her about wearing a bra. She turned to the group and asked innocently, "Do you have the time?" Then she walked away! The group was so surprised by her question that they stopped teasing her, giving her a chance to get away.

5. Find a friend to hook up with.

I'm sure you've heard the phrase, "safety in numbers." Teasers are less likely to tease you if you are with a friend. They're even less likely to tease you if you're with a bunch of friends. Encourage your child to buddy up with another child, especially when the teaser is around.

6. Avoid your teasers.

It may seem obvious that you should avoid your teasers, but some children try to directly take on their teasers by teasing them back or provoking them into more teasing. Teach your child to stay away from teasers. Encourage him to hang around kids who are positive and have "good friend" qualities.

7. Acknowledge mistakes and move on.

This is especially useful if your child is teased for making a mistake during a sporting event or while answering a question in school. Remind your child that everybody makes mistakes. Mistakes help us learn. Your child can practice responding to errors by saying, "You're right. I blew it. I'll get it right next time."

8. Articulate the obvious.

If someone is provoking your child, tell your child to simply point out, without judgment, what the other child is doing that is bothering him. Rather than saying, "Stop it! You're annoying me," say instead, "You are kicking my chair." By saying the obvious without judgment, you give the provocative child the chance to save face and stop kicking.

9. Perfect a dirty look.

You might need to sit down in front of a mirror and practice with your child giving a dirty look. Some children have such angelic faces, it's hard to imagine them giving anyone a dirty look! But for those children who are not very verbal or who feel uncomfortable with a verbal comeback, a smirk or a dirty look can be just as powerful as words. It's all in the attitude. Work with your child on developing a confident attitude. Give your child lots of encouragement for his efforts.

10. Confront whispering directly.

Part of the power of whispering is that it is underhanded and indirect. By challenging it directly with, "Do you have something you want to say to me?" your child doesn't allow the whispering to go on without comment. Children who whisper do so partly because they assume no one will call them on it. Confronting the behavior directly and without emotion often puts an end to the whispering.

11. Learn miscellaneous comebacks.

For a younger child, you may need to teach him specific responses to say to a teaser. Older children will have an easier time coming up with words on the spot. Keep in mind that some children are just not "comeback" kids. If these kids get into a comeback war with a teaser, they are definitely going to lose. So for these kids, it's essential that they learn to walk away after they've delivered a comeback. Other more timid children may do better with a dirty look or hooking up with a friend. Don't try to make your child a comeback kid if it doesn't feel comfortable to him. Work with your child's temperament to find the technique that works best for him.

Review the following comeback statements and have your child come up with ones of his own. He may have an easier time remembering and delivering his own comebacks than trying to memorize the ones listed below.

Comebacks

"Are you enjoying yourself, because I'm not?"

"Oh well, what can I say? You've said it all."

"So."

"What ever."

"That's a good one."

"Yeah, right."

"Really?"

"Say what?"

"You're kidding. Right?"

"Let me know when you get to the funny part."

12. Move toward an adult.

Tattling is generally a big "no no" in a teasing situation. I don't encourage tattling unless a child is being emotionally harassed or physically threatened. A child who tattles becomes the target of teasers. But a reasonable alternative is for your child to move in the direction of an adult. On the playground, for instance, there is usually an adult monitor your child can stand or play near. Teasers are less likely to tease when an adult is present, and they won't view your child as a tattletale.

When Parents Need To Get Involved

Once children understand the types of teasing, what behaviors cause them to get teased, and nonviolent techniques for dealing with teasing, teasing usually dissipates. However, some children are not getting teased so much as they're being bullied. Bullying can be defined as any of the following behaviors:

▸ Physical aggression

▸ Social alienation

▸ Emotional and verbal aggression

▸ Intimidation

Bullying behavior is very destructive to a child. Bullies do not stop when your child asks them to stop. The bully's behavior is ritualistic and sadistic. A bully's way of relating to another child is through domination.

Children who are victims of bullying tend to suffer from low self-esteem, anxiety, school phobia, and poor academic performance. It's crucial that you get involved if you suspect that your child is being bullied. Keep your eyes open for any of the following bullying behaviors.

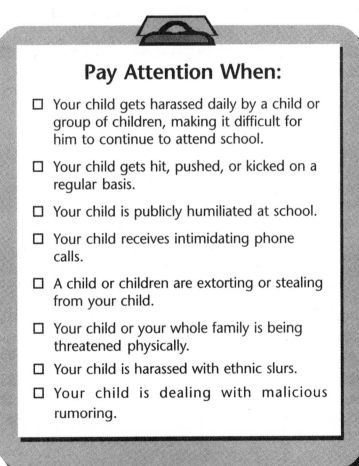

Pay Attention When:

☐ Your child gets harassed daily by a child or group of children, making it difficult for him to continue to attend school.

☐ Your child gets hit, pushed, or kicked on a regular basis.

☐ Your child is publicly humiliated at school.

☐ Your child receives intimidating phone calls.

☐ A child or children are extorting or stealing from your child.

☐ Your child or your whole family is being threatened physically.

☐ Your child is harassed with ethnic slurs.

☐ Your child is dealing with malicious rumoring.

Steps To Take

| Step One | **Talk to your child's teacher.** |

Don't blame or attack the teacher, rather find out if the teacher notices anything going on. If not, ask the teacher to keep an eye on the situation for you. If the teacher does not want to get involved, go to the school psychologist, guidance counselor, or social worker. If you still aren't getting help, meet with the principal to discuss the school's policy on bullying.

| Step Two | **Make sure your child hangs out with friends.** |

Bullies are less likely to bother your child when he is with others. Identify the times when the bullying is happening and round up friends to be with your child at those times.

| Step Three | **Boost your child's self-esteem.** |

Remind your child how brave he is to have faced the bullies, and that you understand how hard it is for him to keep going to school when he's being bullied.

| Step Four | **Educate your child.** |

Explain to your child why kids bully other kids. Help him to understand that the bully is the one with the problem, and that the bully is unhappy and feels powerless and that's why he bullies.

| Step Five | **Tell your child to refuse the bullies' demands.** |

Bullies like kids who are obedient or easily intimidated.

Role-play with your child ways to refuse the bullies demands. If the bullying occurs outside, you may have to encourage your child to run away, go toward an adult, or even run to a stranger's doorway. This may feel to your child like he's giving in, but that's not the case. Your child's safety is of utmost importance. Reframe your child's actions as active rather than passive.

Step Six *Go to the PTA.*

If the bullying problem seems widespread, you can bring up the issue to other parents at a PTA meeting. Parents can be great resources for each other. They also can help break up cliques by speaking to their own children.

Step Seven *Get community support.*

You might suggest that a social skills program be offered at your school to help children learn conflict resolution and problem-solving skills.

What To Do If Your Child Is a Bully

More often than not, parents of bullies do not realize their children are bullies. If you're getting reports from other parents and from teachers that your child is bullying other children, you need to accept that reality. It's very hard to acknowledge that your child is being mean to others. You may be tempted to see the school as the problem or to believe that your child is just defending himself. If you get reports from more than one source over a period of time that your child is bullying other kids, you need to pay attention and take action.

Steps To Take

Step One	**Take the problem seriously.**

Step Two	**Set limits and consequences for your child to help him understand the impact he has on others.**

Step Three	**Try to avoid having long, drawn out conversations with your child about why he bullies.**

Instead, focus entirely on the behavior itself and appropriate alternatives to it.

Step Four	**Supervise your child more closely.**

Step Five	**Teach your child good problem-solving methods.**

Refer to Chapter Eight of this book.

Step Six	**Reward and praise positive social behavior whenever you witness it.**

Step Seven	*Provide your child with opportunities to help others.*

Step Eight	*Look for problems that may be underlying your child's behavior.*

Is your child being bullied himself? Are there other areas of your child's life where he feels helpless and insecure? He may be seeking feelings of power by making other kids feel helpless.

Step Nine	*Take a very close look at your own family relationships.*

Are there open lines of communication between family members? Don't use the "boys will be boys" explanation and praise your child for being tough. Instead, encourage appropriate expression of feelings and the development of good listening skills.

Step Ten	*Give your child alternative outlets to discharge aggression.*

For instance, try contact sports or karate.

Step Eleven	*Consider seeking professional help to aid your child in building healthy give-and-take relationships with other children.*

Teasing Games and Exercises

1. Finish the Comic Strip

Develop a comic strip with your child, showing a "teaser" and "teasee." Leave the last frame blank. Ask your child to finish the comic strip using appropriate responses.

2. Role-play

Role-play with your child, allowing him to play the role of both the "teaser" and "teasee." Try out various coping techniques. See which ones work best for your child.

3. The Mirror Game

Help your child practice the appropriate facial expressions, body language, and posture to cope with teasing.

4. Videotape

Videotape your child's responses to teasing. Play back the tape for him so he can choose which response works best for him.

Chapter Seven

MANAGING STRESS

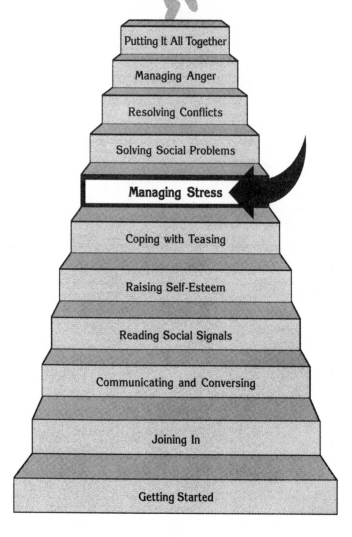

Putting It All Together

Managing Anger

Resolving Conflicts

Solving Social Problems

Managing Stress

Coping with Teasing

Raising Self-Esteem

Reading Social Signals

Communicating and Conversing

Joining In

Getting Started

GOALS ▸

In this chapter, you will learn how to help your child:

✔ Understand what stresses him.

✔ Manage stress more effectively.

✔ Learn relaxation methods.

✔ Reduce physical manifestations of stress (temper outbursts, stomachaches, nightmares, and so on).

Jason

*J*ason is an active, bright, well-liked ten-year-old who enjoys doing many things. He loves school and does well in his classes. He plays several sports, including soccer, baseball, and basketball, and participates in the Boy Scouts. Jason's parents are active in the local church, and Jason not only attends services with his family every Sunday, but also he participates in the church's youth group. By the middle of his school year, Jason's behavior starts changing. He is beginning to act cranky and talk back to his parents. He wants to quit playing basketball and he complains a lot about being tired. His grades are slipping and his teacher has expressed concern about Jason's change of attitude. Jason's parents bring him to the pediatrician, who finds nothing wrong with Jason. When they bring him to a psychotherapist, they're told that Jason is overcommitted and stressed out. His parents decide to cut back on some of Jason's activities.

Samantha

Samantha is an eight-year-old third-grade student at a small parochial school. She is a bright, fun-loving girl with lots of friends and a cheerful outlook. Unfortunately, Samantha has trouble in class. She has difficulty understanding the directions given to her by the teacher, and she can't seem to focus on her schoolwork while in class, which annoys the other kids and the teacher. Samantha's parents had her evaluated privately and Samantha was diagnosed as having Attention-Deficit Disorder (ADD) and auditory learning disabilities, which makes school challenging for her. The teacher has begun sending notes home to Samantha's parents, saying that Samantha is not working up to her potential, is disruptive in class, and is mean to her classmates. The teacher is unwilling to make special accommodations for Samantha's disabilities because she believes that Samantha can do the work, but she just doesn't want to. This angers Samantha's parents. They want their daughter to switch to a different classroom with a teacher who will be more understanding of Samantha's struggles. Even though Samantha thinks her teacher hates her and finds her stupid, she wants to remain in class with her friends.

Stress is common in the lives of children, just as it is in our adult lives. And, just as for adults, stress can come from a variety of sources. Jason is a classic case of an overscheduled child whose stress comes from a lack of "down time." As our lives become more hectic, our children often become caught up in the same frantic pace. Samantha, on the other hand, experiences stress as a result of the special challenges associated with learning disabilities. There is a large gap between what she needs in her learning environment and what her teachers are able to offer her.

The Stress Management Quiz

Use the following quiz to determine if your child needs help managing stress:

☐ Does your child frequently exhibit physical ailments: pounding or rapid heartbeat, headaches, stomach problems, poor appetite, and so on?

☐ Does he have nightmares?

☐ Does he have trouble falling asleep or staying asleep?

☐ Is your child irritable?

☐ Does he exhibit compulsive behavior (nail biting, hand washing, lip licking, repetitive facial movements)?

☐ Does your child cry frequently?

☐ Does he show continued signs of fatique?

☐ Does your child have poor concentration?

☐ Does your child have "accidents"?

If you answered *no* to all of these questions, your child may manage his stress well. You can skip over this chapter for now and come back to it later if your child begins to show signs of stress.

The Reality of Childhood Stress

When we reflect on childhood, we often think of it as a care-free time compared to adulthood. We can't help but think that kids have it easier. We're wrong. The average child experiences stress on a regular basis. Kids define feeling stressed as "being stuck in a feeling of upset," "wanting to cry all the time," or "feeling like my guts are going to explode." For some children, school is filled with such stressful situations that they dread getting on the school bus each morning.

All children are stressed by change and uncertainty in their lives. For preschoolers, separation issues can be very painful. For example, a preschooler will likely feel stressed if his mother returns to the work force after being at home for several years. For kindergartners, a trip to the doctor or being left to play at a friend's house might be stressful. And for an elementary school child, the pressure to succeed academically and socially is enormous. We can see in Samantha's case that the pressures of school are affecting her greatly. Having been diagnosed with ADD, she is aware that she is different from her peers, and she reacts to this by lashing out and provoking those around her.

In addition to normal developmental stressors, children also face temporarily stressful situations. Many children are exposed to parental conflict, separation, divorce, and custody battles. Children are more mobile today, changing schools or moving from one home to another. They frequently must adjust to new neighborhoods and new classmates. In general, kids are not in charge of their own destinies, and as parents make most of the decisions for them, kids end up feeling out of control. More and more children are being left in the care of professionals while both parents work outside the home. Stressed out and overburdened parents unwittingly create a frenetic home environment, making it hard for them to identify stress in their own kids. What's more, some children also must cope with a serious illness in the family or the death of a close relative. There is little emotional energy left in families to deal with these catastrophic problems because the energy has already been used up dealing with daily life.

> ### Stress Makers
>
> ▸ Being overscheduled—not enough "down time"
>
> ▸ Having homework that is either too hard or too much
>
> ▸ Feeling that parents' expectations are unrealistic
>
> ▸ Being yelled at by parents or teachers
>
> ▸ Feeling left out at school
>
> ▸ Dealing with peer pressure
>
> ▸ Wanting to be perfect
>
> ▸ Having parents who work too much

Stress In Your Child

The first step in helping your child is to determine whether your child is experiencing stress. Look for certain behavioral clues, and keep in mind your child's unique history and personality. It's more important to notice any changes in behavior rather than just the behavior itself. Ask yourself the following questions:

1. How long have these symptoms lasted?

If you have a child who has never been a good sleeper, for example, it's less likely that his sleep problems are caused by stress. On the other hand, if your child suddenly begins waking up in the middle of the night, crying and complaining of nightmares, then you need to consider stress as a possible cause. In addition, if a symptom persists for a few days, it may not be caused by stress, but if it lasts for more than a few weeks, you need to take notice.

2. How intense are the symptoms?

It's okay for your child to complain of a stomachache before school, as long as he goes to school and comes home without further complaint. But if he says he can't get out of bed because of his stomachache and begins missing school because of his complaints, then you should take him to the doctor. If your child complains of a stomachache before school and then, as soon as he is allowed to stay home, he appears healthy and has no further complaints, this may be a sign of stress. You have relieved the stress by allowing him to stay home from school. Find out what it is about school that is stressing him.

3. Do other kids his age have the same symptoms?

It's okay if your two-year-old has trouble staying in his seat at a restaurant, but it's not okay if your eight-year-old has trouble. It's acceptable for your three-year-old to have difficulty separating from you, but it's not acceptable for your ten-year-old. Check with your pediatrician if you're unsure of what is developmentally appropriate for your child.

4. How many symptoms are there?

Stress often causes more than one symptom at a time. If we look at Jason's situation, we see that he complained about fatigue *and* he was becoming irritable *and* he was withdrawing from activities which had previously been fun for him. This combination of behaviors led his parents to recognize his stress.

Symptoms of Stress in Children

☐ Physical ailments: uneven heartbeat, shallow breathing, teeth grinding, teeth clenching, frequent urination, headaches, stomach problems, restlessness, skin blemishes or rashes, and poor appetite or other changes in eating habits

☐ Nightmares

☐ Insomnia

☐ Irritability

☐ Compulsive behavior (nail biting, hand washing, lip licking)

☐ Bragging

☐ Shyness

☐ Poor concentration

☐ Nervous laughter

☐ General anxiety

☐ Fatigue

☐ Frequent crying

Helping Your Child Reduce Stress

You can teach your child basic stress-management techniques to help him handle stress. The following methods are useful for children of all ages. Some of these techniques require your guidance —you'll need to talk through an exercise or activity with your child. Not all of these techniques will be right for your child. Try those that feel comfortable for you.

Stress and Homework

Step One *Take baby steps.*

Help your child break down what needs to be accomplished into small, manageable steps. For example, "For your math homework, just do the first five problems. I'll check them over when you're done and then we'll go on to the next set of problems."

Step Two *Schedule breaks.*

Reward your child in little ways during his homework breaks. Let him get a drink. Give him a hug.

Step Three *Set realistic expectations for your child.*

Be aware of your child's capabilities and limitations. You want your child to be challenged, not overwhelmed.

Step	**Make sure the TV or computer is a**
Four	**stress reliever, not a stress enhancer.**

Just because your child wants to watch TV or play on the computer does not mean that your child needs to do these things. Many TV and computer programs are violent and competitive, which can increase your child's stress level rather than decrease it. Keep your child away from too much of these activities, particularly if they are violent in nature. Help your child use TV and computer for educational purposes.

Stress and the Family

Step	**Set up a special time each day**
One	**to spend with your child alone.**

Start with 15 minutes or so. Follow your child's lead. If he doesn't feel like talking and would rather just play cards, then do what he wants. He may talk to you when you least expect it.

Step	**Think of things that your child**
Two	**is proud of, and emphasize them.**

This helps combat perfectionism and low self-esteem. Know your child's strengths, and let him know that you know.

Step Three	**Have a family meeting once a week.**

Sunday evening can be a good night to have a family meal without distractions and share positive feelings about each other. This is also a good time to solve family problems.

Step Four	*Successfully manage your own stress.*

Cut back at work, if possible, to be more available to your children. Avoid walking into the house when you're stressed out—try to leave work behind at the office. If you can, stop at the gym after work to relieve your own stress before you come home at the end of the day.

Step Five	*Don't use your child as your therapist.*

Keep your problems to yourself. Talk with your spouse or friends about your personal problems, not with your child. Children can't handle the role of being a parent's confidante. They feel stressed by their inability to help you.

Stress and Your Child's Social Life

Step One	*Make sure your child is not overcommitted.*

Free play is the work of childhood. We need to allow time for unscheduled play so that children can relax. See to it that your child has time at home just to "do his own thing." Jason's parents learned that their son was "running on empty" and needed time just to do nothing, so they scaled back his commitments. Prioritize your child's activities and drop ones that are less important.

Step Two | *Be proactive against social stress.*

Come up with a plan to deal with potentially stressful situations ahead of time. Sit down with your child before a new activity occurs that might be stressful, and formulate and rehearse a plan. For example, Samantha's parents might say to her, "You are going to a new class today. What can you do if you don't understand what the teacher is telling you?" "I can write down my questions and at the end of class, I can ask my teacher the questions." "Good idea! Let's try that today. I'll ask you about it when you get home from school."

Step Three | *Seek spiritual support.*

If you gain strength and support from spirituality,

establish and strengthen your ties to that community.

Youth groups can be a nice way for your child to socialize and receive support.

Stress and Your Child's Body

Step One	*Make sure your child eats and sleeps well.*

Feed your child healthy, nutritious meals and snacks. Stress depletes essential nutrients from our bodies. Give your child regular bedtimes to ensure that he gets enough sleep for his age. Ask your pediatrician how much sleep your child should be getting.

Step Two	*Get physical.*

Any organized or individual sport—running, walking, biking, or karate—will help reduce body tension associated with stress. Stretch all the major muscle groups. Instead of just sitting and watching television, your child can stretch out while he watches.

Stress and Your Child's Feelings

Step One	*Teach your child "positive self-talk."*

When your child thinks negatively about something, encourage him to replace those negative thoughts with positive ones. For example, if your child is thinking, "I can't do it, I'm afraid," encourage him to think, "I'm okay, it's going to go fine."

Step Two	*Bring humor into your child's life.*

Go to a comedy show with your child. Rent a funny video and watch it together. Read a joke book. And don't forget to laugh at yourself.

| Step Three | *Encourage your child to express anger with words, not actions.* |

Unresolved anger can be a potent source of stress. It's not whether you feel angry, but how you express it that's important. Practice with your child verbal ways of expressing anger. "I get angry when you . . ." "That makes me mad!" If your child feels the need to vent physically, let him punch a punching bag or a pillow.

| Step Four | **Write a "Worry List."** |

When there is too much to do in one day, help your child develop a list that notes each task in order of importance and what needs to be done. When tasks have been completed, check them off the list.

Sample Worry List:

▸ Do my homework
▸ Clean my room
▸ Feed the dog
▸ Practice the piano

Stress-Reduction Games and Exercises

1. Deep breathing

Teach your child to breathe slowly and rhythmically, in through his nose and out through his mouth. This will slow down the heart rate and lead to an overall state of relaxation. A good time to practice this is right before your child goes to sleep at night.

2. Visual imagery

Think of this as "relaxing daydreaming." Your child should close his eyes and perhaps imagine a pleasant trip, a major accomplishment, or a favorite memory.

3. Muscle massage

Give your child a nightly massage. This will help him relax and go to sleep.

4. The back tickle

Gently stroke your child's back. This is a good technique for children who don't like full back massages.

5. The body shake

Have your child jump up and down and wiggle his limbs to shake the physical tension from his body.

6. Progressive relaxation

Have your child systematically tense and relax all major muscles. Since stress causes muscle tightness, this exercise should help your child feel less stressed.

Chapter Eight

SOLVING SOCIAL PROBLEMS

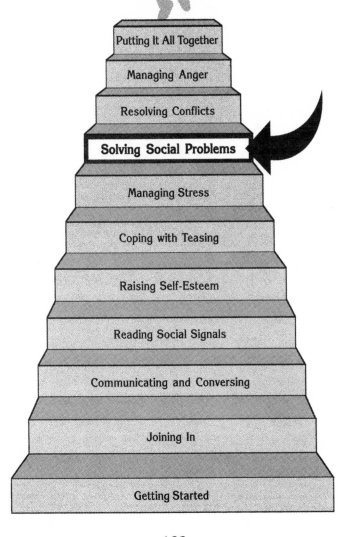

Putting It All Together

Managing Anger

Resolving Conflicts

Solving Social Problems

Managing Stress

Coping with Teasing

Raising Self-Esteem

Reading Social Signals

Communicating and Conversing

Joining In

Getting Started

GOALS ▶

In this chapter, you will learn how to help
your child:

✓ Come up with several possible solutions to
problems.

✓ Predict short- and long-term consequences
of behavior.

✓ Develop effective strategies to solve social
problems.

✓ Think before acting.

✓ Develop plans and backup plans as solutions to problems.

Patrick

*E*leven-year-old Patrick comes home almost every day after
school with the same complaint: "I hate Ryan! He is always bugging me in class when I'm trying to get my work
done." When Patrick's dad asks him for more details, Patrick
says Ryan kicks his chair, giggles in his ear, blurts out answers to questions, and messes with the stuff on Patrick's desk.
When Dad asks Patrick how he handles Ryan's behavior,
Patrick says, "I tell him to stop, but it doesn't work." Both Dad
and Mom try to tell Patrick other ways to deal with Ryan, but
Patrick doesn't seem to want to listen. He is pretty stuck on
just saying "stop"—he can't seem to switch gears and think of
alternative ways to solve the problem. Patrick's parents feel
unable to help their son since Patrick seems unwilling to accept their advice.

Shannon

Seven-year-old Shannon's best defense is an offense. If a child gets too close to Shannon on the playground, she kicks her. If another child takes a toy away from Shannon, she grabs back the toy and shoves her. Shannon is happy with the results of her actions because, in the short term, she gets what she wants—the return of her toy. But she has trouble seeing how her behavior affects her in the long term. The other kids in class avoid her. They think she is mean and are afraid she might hurt them. Shannon's teachers and her parents have tried to help her see the error of her ways, but Shannon doesn't have the skills necessary to handle these situations smoothly and effectively.

Patrick and Shannon are experiencing social problems that they can't seem to resolve on their own. They don't have the skills to figure out an effective solution. Children often have trouble thinking of several possible solutions to problems. They get stuck in reacting automatically, using the same approach to every situation, even though it may not be the best approach. Shannon tends to react with aggression first, not thinking about the consequences of her actions. Patrick becomes frustrated when his ineffective solution doesn't work.

The Problem-Solving Quiz

Use the following quiz to determine if your child needs help building problem-solving skills:

☐ Is your child able to see his own role in a social problem?

☐ Does your child take responsibility for his own social mistakes?

☐ Is your child able to put himself in the other person's shoes?

☐ Can your child think of a variety of solutions to social problems?

☐ Does your child follow through with a thoughtful plan of action to solve his problems?

☐ Can your child anticipate others' responses to him?

☐ Can your child imagine long-term consequences to actions?

☐ Can your child imagine short-term consequences to actions?

☐ Does your child speak openly about his problems?

☐ Is your child able to set goals for himself, and then take the steps necessary to achieve these goals?

If you answered *yes* to all of these questions, your child is an excellent problem-solver already, so you can just skip over this chapter. If you answered *no* to some of them, it would be worthwhile for you to continue reading and try some of the exercises in this chapter.

Six Simple Steps To Solving Social Problems

The steps required to solve problems are easy. Getting your child to talk to you about his problems, and then helping him solve them on his own, is not so easy. The basic steps are as follows:

Step One | *Figure out what the problem is.*

Step Two | *Brainstorm several solutions to the problem.*

Step Three | *Think about the consequences of each solution.*

Step Four | *Develop a plan of action.*

Step Five | *Develop a backup plan.*

Step Six | *Try out both your plan and backup plan.*

Problem-Solving Snafus

The above steps may seem easy, but kids with social issues can have lots of difficulty solving problems. Perhaps you've heard your child make statements like these:

▶ **"I don't like talking about my problems."**

It's very hard to help your child with a problem if he won't talk to you about it. Getting some children to open up is like pulling teeth. Denying the problem can sometimes make it worse because nothing is being done to correct the situation.

▶ **"I don't like to think before I react to problems."**

Many children react to problems instinctively. They choose the actions that first come into their heads. These are usually the impulsive behaviors that get them into trouble. For instance, Shannon's impulse is to "kick first, think later." One of the challenges of problem-solving is to help your child slow down and think before reacting.

▶ **"I can only think of one way to solve this problem."**

It takes considerable effort to generate many possible solutions to a given problem. Patrick, for example, can think of only one thing to do to stop Ryan, and he keeps doing it, even though it's not working. The first solutions that come to mind tend to be the impulsive ones. But it's the thoughtful solutions that are more effective and long lasting.

▶ **"I don't care what happens later. I want the problem fixed now!"**

It's clear in Shannon's case that when she kicks a child, she doesn't care what the child will think of her in the long-term, she just wants what she wants, *now*. Helping your child understand how destructive long-term consequences can be is a challenging, but highly useful, goal in problem-solving.

▶ **"I can't remember what to do when the problem comes up again."**

Without regular practice and role-playing, your child may forget how to solve the problem when faced with it directly.

Helping Your Child Solve His Own Problems

 Step One | *Ask your child gently about the problem.*

See if your child feels like talking. "You seem upset. Do you want to talk about it?" If your child resists talking, reassure him that you are there for him if he feels like talking at another time. "If you feel like talking later, I'll be in the kitchen making dinner."

Step Two	**Listen to your child without judgment.**

Find a quiet place and time to talk with your child. Allow him as much time as he needs to speak. Listen to the whole story before responding. Use active-listening skills by making supportive statements. Open-ended statements are much less threatening to children than questions. Try saying, "Tell me what happened," or "Tell me all about it," rather than, "Why did you do that?" You may be tempted at times to respond emotionally to your child, especially if you do not agree with his actions. Stay calm. Avoid reacting. Remain supportive.

Step Three **Use your reflective listening skills.**

Periodically reflect back what you have heard your child say to make sure you understand his feelings and thoughts. Allow him to correct you if you don't have it quite right. "So, what I hear you saying is that Jimmy keeps kicking your chair in class and it upsets you?"

Step Four	**Encourage your child to sum up the problem in two sentences or less.**

Having a clear, succinct understanding of the problem will help your child find appropriate solutions.

Step Five	**Let your child come up with all kinds of solutions to the problem.**

Keep in mind that the first one or two ideas will probably be the less productive, more impulsive ones. But don't judge any responses. Treat each solution, no matter how seemingly impractical, with the utmost respect. Write down the solutions as your child comes up with them. Respond enthusiastically to all of them. "That's an idea. What's another idea?" Avoid coming up with the solutions yourself. If your child says, "I can't think of any solutions," or "I've tried *all* the solutions and none of them work," or "I don't know how to solve this problem," don't accept it! Sit patiently and confidently, waiting for him to come up with some solutions. "I know you can do it. I'll wait until you come up with something. We've got plenty of time."

Step Six	***Help your child evaluate the strengths and weaknesses of his ideas.***

Ask your child, "What would happen if you did that?" Help him to understand both the negative and the positive consequences of his choices. Remember to consider both the short- and the long-term consequences of his solutions. For instance, if your child punches another classmate when he gets teased, the classmate might stop teasing him in the short-term, but the long-term consequence is that your child will get in trouble and be seen as a "hothead."

Step Seven	***Help your child develop a plan of action.***

After your child has had a chance to consider the consequences of his solutions, encourage him to choose a solution that works for him. Keep in mind that your way of handling a situation may not be the same as your child's. Allow him the right to choose his own solution to the problem so that he'll be more invested in the plan. Since your child has already ruled out the "poor risk" solutions, he is ready to develop a step-by-step approach to the problem. Imagine how good he'll feel when you encourage him to make his own choices. It may help to write down your child's plan of action, and then to role-play or rehearse his idea. Anticipate with your child potential problems that may arise in the interaction, and practice with him ahead of time ways to cope with obstacles as they come up.

Step Eight **Choose a backup plan.**

It's always a good idea to come up with a second choice, and even a third choice, in case the first one is unsuccessful. In the same way that you choose and rehearse the primary plan, do the same with a backup plan. It's better to have your child overequipped with solutions, rather than leave him with too few tools in a given situation.

Step Nine **Check in with your child.**

Make sure you ask your child how the problem-solving solution worked. "You said yesterday you were going to say 'So!' if Katey teased you today. Did you have a chance to use your solution?" Give your child lots of encouragement if he used the solution, and if he didn't, review the solution again and encourage him to use it the next time. If your child forgot to use the solution, you may need to review it and role-play again so the plan is fresh in his mind.

Your child will continue to face problems as he goes through life, but equipping him with problem-solving skills will pave the way for him to cope effectively with issues as they arise. You will notice that the problem-solving skills in this chapter are used in later chapters, as well.

Conflict resolution and anger control strategies are based on the foundation of problem-solving skills. The steps learned here are fundamental and can be used in any situation. As your child becomes more comfortable thinking about problems and how to solve them, he will become increasingly proficient at navigating his way through challenging social situations.

The Birthday Party—
A Great Place To Learn About
Problem-Solving and Cooperation

A birthday party can be a wonderful forum for reinforcing problem-solving skills through cooperative games and activities. You can create an atmosphere where the focus is on working together to achieve a common goal, ensuring a positive experience for all of the children in attendance.

In cooperative activities, there are no winners and losers—everyone is a winner. Team-building games promote trust, self-confidence, and the development of healthy peer relationships. The essential ingredient to successful cooperative play at a birthday party is adult supervision. With adult input, cooperative activities will reap positive social benefits for children in a way that other activities can't.

Establish a Positive Atmosphere

If you are a party-giver, you'll want to do everything you can to establish a positive atmosphere—one in which healthy cooperation can take place. Keep in mind the following pointers during the preparation and execution of the party:

1. Reward the entire group of children for any positive interaction.

For example, if everyone participates in a cooperative way, then everyone gets a special trinket or snack.

2. Be flexible.

Alter your plans for the party at a moment's notice to meet the needs of the kids.

3. If the children become restless or bored during an activity, shift focus.

Play a simple game to bring the focus back to the group.

4. Use "I" messages to correct any misbehavior.

For example, you might say, "Susie, I can't hear John when there is so much noise in here."

5. Dispense rules and reprimands in a positive way.

Instead of saying, "Don't spill your milk," say "Let's push your milk away from the edge of the table so it won't spill."

6. Focus the games on enjoyment, fun, and strategizing.

Minimize the emphasis on winning and losing.

7. Emphasize self-improvement and self-correction, rather than competition.

8. Avoid the "last one picked" syndrome.

Choose well-balanced teams yourself, or stop after half of the kids are chosen and choose the rest of the teams yourself. You also can choose teams easily and fairly by picking names out of a hat.

9. Develop strategies for attending to two or more children at once.

"What a team! Your group works so well together!"

10. If you spot a child who appears left out, give him a leadership role to play.

11. Encourage the children to reach their personal best rather than compare themselves to the other children.

Emphasize self-improvement. Make sure any competition is against the child's past performance rather than another child's performance.

12. Avoid eliminating children from the game.

13. Emphasize the fun and enjoyment of just playing the game rather than rewarding the children with trophies or prizes.

Play Games That Encourage Problem-Solving

Following are some games and activities that children can play at an indoor or outdoor party. Keep in mind that these activities require an adult for coordination and supervision.

1. Human Tangle

Instruct the kids to stand in a circle, shoulder to shoulder. Have them put both their arms in the center of the circle and hold hands with someone across from them. Make sure that no one holds both hands with the same person or holds hands with the person next to him. Keeping hands held together, the group needs to work as a team and use decision-making and problem-solving skills to try to get untangled.

2. The Puzzle Hunt

Prepare a jigsaw puzzle for each player by cutting magazine covers and postcards into pieces. Hide all but one piece of each puzzle in a room. When the children arrive, give each child the single puzzle piece. They must help each other find all the pieces and put all the puzzles back together.

3. The Spider's Web

You need a lot of string and enough small prizes for everyone. Fasten a string to each of the gifts. Hide the gifts in various places in a room, winding the string around furniture and banisters as you go. Each person is given the end of a string and must figure out how to untangle it to find the prize. Each child who finishes must help the others find their prizes.

4. Celebrity Pairs

This takes a little preparation. Prepare a stack of index

cards. Each card should be one half of a famous pair (for example, Batman of Batman and Robin). Tape the cards randomly on the children's backs. Ask them to find their other halves by asking yes or no questions—they can't simply ask, "Who am I?" For instance, they might ask, "Am I a cartoon character?" or "Am I an action figure?" They have to use problem-solving strategies to figure out who they are before they can find out who their partner is.

5. Blanket Ball

Ask each child to hold an end of a large blanket so that it lies flat between them. Place a large, lightweight ball in the middle of the blanket. The group's goal is to figure out how to cooperatively move the blanket up and down so that the ball will fly into a nearby trash can.

6. The Alligator Pond

The group will use two wooden boards as a "bridge" to get from the start position to the finish position. If a person falls off the board at any time, the whole group must return to the start position and begin again. Encourage all members to concentrate to work together, and to brainstorm their solutions to get from start to finish.

Problem-Solving
Games and Exercises

1. The Problem-Solving Worksheet

Develop a problem-solving log. Help your child create a journal to track and evaluate his problem-solving abilities.

The following is a sample problem-solving log:

This problem had to do with (circle):

Teasing	Self-esteem
Joining in	Talking and listening
Problem solving	Dealing with siblings
Peer pressure	Resolving conflicts with others
Anger control	Resolving conflicts with parents
Other _____	

What did the other person think or feel?

_____

_____

_____

_____

Were there any ways that you might have contributed to the problem? What were they?

_____

_____

_____

_____

Did you brainstorm different ways to deal with the situation? What were your options?

_____

_____

_____

_____

Did you think about consequences?
(what might happen)   ☐ Yes   ☐ No

_____

_____

_____

_____

What did you decide to do about the situation?

Rate yourself:

☐   I didn't think of any solutions

☐   I only thought of one solution

☐   I thought of many solutions and I tried one

☐   It did not work

☐   It worked!

_____

_____

_____

_____

_____

2. The Brainstorming Game

Develop your brainstorming muscles. Choose an everyday object, like a paper clip or a chalkboard eraser. Explain to your child how easy it is to think only of one or two uses for these common objects. Then ask your child to brainstorm other possible uses for them. Write down these ideas, no matter how silly they may seem. Continue to write until he runs out of ideas. This activity helps your child flex his brainstorming muscles to encourage freedom of thought in finding solutions to problems.

3. The Problem-Solving Game

Play a problem-solving game. Create a group of sample situation cards marked with common problems children experience. Using any game board you have at home, allow your child to roll the dice and pick a card. If he answers the problem appropriately, give him a poker chip and allow him to move the number shown on the dice. The following are sample problem situations:

▸ Someone on your bus calls you names all the time. What do you do?

▸ You are playing basketball with a friend who keeps hogging the ball. What can you do?

▸ Your mom cleaned your room and now you can't find your favorite toy. What can you do?

▸ Two kids who sit behind you in class keep talking and you can't hear the teacher. What can you do?

▸ You turn on the TV. You and your sister want to watch different shows. What can you do?

▸ You get a "C" on your report card and you think you deserve a better grade. What can you do?

▸ Your teacher blames you for talking when it was really the kid sitting next to you. He denies it. You get in trouble. What can you do?

Feel free to make up situations that are particularly relevant to your child's life.

Chapter Nine

RESOLVING CONFLICTS

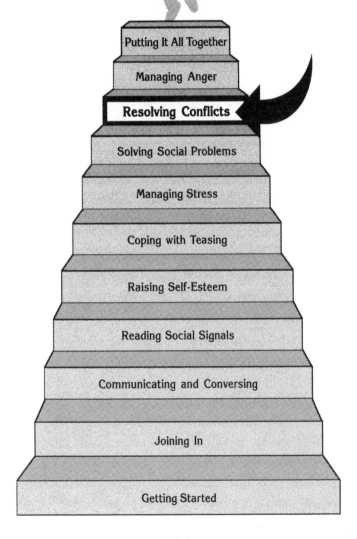

Putting It All Together

Managing Anger

Resolving Conflicts

Solving Social Problems

Managing Stress

Coping with Teasing

Raising Self-Esteem

Reading Social Signals

Communicating and Conversing

Joining In

Getting Started

GOALS ▸

In this chapter, you will learn how to help your child:

✔ Argue fairly and effectively.

✔ Understand strategies for negotiation.

✔ Develop the skills necessary to compromise.

✔ Identify behaviors to avoid when arguing.

✔ Express feelings using "I" messages.

✔ Role-play the other's position.

Charlie

C harlie and his dad are always fighting. They seem to constantly push each other's buttons. Dad asks Charlie to do a chore, for example, "Clean up your room!" Charlie says, "I will. In a minute." And the conflict begins. Dad usually resorts to threatening to take away Charlie's Nintendo game. Charlie ends up whining and yelling in frustration. Dad escalates the conflict by lecturing, to which Charlie responds by covering his ears. This leads Dad to yell and to increase his threats by saying things like: "No birthday party"; "No TV for a month"; or "Early bedtime for a year." Dad begins to call Charlie names like "ungrateful," "spoiled brat," and "lazy," to which Charlie responds by crying, screaming, and running to his room and slamming the door.

Alisa

A lisa likes to get her way all the time, especially when she's playing with her friends, Sarah and Liz. As long as the girls are doing things Alisa's way, Alisa is happy. But when

*Sarah or Liz wants to do something a different way, Alisa be-
comes frustrated and tries to get them to do what she wants to
do. She will use every trick in the book. She will tell them that
their idea is stupid. She will raise her voice and threaten not to
be friends with them anymore if they don't do it her way. Alisa
will even use bribery to pit one girl against the other. The play
date usually ends in one of two ways: either the girls give in
and do it Alisa's way, or Alisa storms off in a huff and refuses
to play with them anymore (until tomorrow, when the same
scenario happens again).*

✏ The Conflict Resolution Quiz

Everyone can use guidance on resolving arguments effectively, even adults. But some children require more
assistance than others do. Use the following quiz to see if
your child needs help resolving conflicts fairly and effectively.

☐ Does your child rarely get into arguments with peers?

☐ Does your child rarely get into arguments at home?

☐ Is your child able to use "I feel" statements to express his feelings?

☐ Is your child frequently able to come up with compromises to resolve conflicts with others?

☐ Is your child able to understand another person's
perspective on an issue?

☐ Does your child use strategies to solve problems?

☐ Does your child avoid the use of threats, putdowns,
yelling, or whining in an argument with others?

☐ Is your child able to keep his cool when in conflict
with someone?

There are few adults that can answer *yes* to all of the above questions, and even fewer children who can. But if you have one of these rare children, I suggest you simply scan this chapter and move on to the next one.

Arguing Well

We often argue with friends and family members when we're angry, frustrated, or upset about something. Do you ever wonder if arguing in front of your children might negatively affect them? Perhaps you think fighting in front of children could adversely affect their mental health. Maybe you think if children observe their parents fighting, they themselves will become more aggressive. There's no need to worry.

Arguing in itself is not inherently dangerous for your child to observe. It actually presents an opportunity for you, as a parent, to demonstrate to your child how to resolve conflicts successfully—by arguing and coming to a resolution, by working out successful compromises, and by showing a willingness to change your behavior and consider another's perspective.

Disputes between family members can teach children that although two people love and respect each other, they do not always agree. It's important that children see their parents as united in basic child-rearing principles and common values, but they also need to see them as unique individuals with their own opinions.

Fighting is easy. Fighting fairly is not. You may go into an argument intending to resolve the conflict quietly and easily, but in the heat of the moment, you can't seem to stop yourself from getting defensive, lashing out, and saying hurtful things. If this is hard for you as an adult, imagine how challenging it is for your child, who is still struggling with self-control issues and learning to express feelings with words, not actions.

Modeling Good Conflict Resolution Techniques

Conflict resolution is an art form. And it is much more successful when both parties follow certain conflict-resolution guidelines. In order to help your child master these techniques, make sure you are modeling them at home. Whether you are arguing with a spouse or with a child, the following techniques will help you resolve your conflicts smoothly:

Step One *Know what "pushes your buttons."*

If you are aware of what really "gets your goat," then you have some ability to control your reactions. Awareness allows you to anticipate angry feelings that might come up in a specific situation. This awareness gives you a little bit of distance and time to come up with an anger control plan in advance.

Make a list with your child of the situations that get him really upset. Help your child understand what pushes his buttons so that he is better prepared for future conflicts.

Step Two   *Plan before you argue.*

If you know you are upset with someone about something, ask yourself the following questions before you confront the person:

▸ What is my position about this?

▸ What is the other person's point of view?

▸ What would I like to get out of this situation?

▸ What might make both me and the other person happy?

The more you plan ahead, the easier it is to remain calm and clearly state your feelings during a discussion.

Help your child plan ahead, too. If you see that he is moving toward a conflict with a peer or an adult, get involved immediately and review with him the above four questions.

Step Three | *Stick to one problem at a time.*

One of the biggest obstacles to successful conflict resolution is the tendency to "pebble count." Rather than remain focused on the subject at hand, you launch into other issues that you're disgruntled about. Don't do this. Pebble-counting tends to weaken your argument and escalate the conflict rather than resolve it. If you have planned ahead, you are less likely to resort to throwing in other issues to try to bolster your point of view.

If you notice your child jumping from subject to subject during an argument, help him get back on the subject. Don't allow yourself to be redirected by irrelevant information. You could say, "That may be important, but we are not talking about that right now. Let's get back to the issue."

Step Four | *Choose the right time and place.*

It's best to resolve conflicts when there are few distractions. Dinnertime with five kids at the table may not be the best time to have a productive discussion. Choose a time when the person you have a conflict with is in a good mood and appears willing to speak openly.

Timing is critical when addressing conflicts with children. Right after school, when they are tired and relieved to be home, is not a good time. Neither is right before school. Try to talk when it is quiet and no one is rushing out the door, perhaps after dinner or before bedtime. Choose a time and place that works best for both you and your child.

| Step Five | *Be direct in saying what you need and feel.* |

This can be particularly difficult for girls who have been socialized to be indirect in getting what they need. Rather than beating around the bush, be direct and open. "I'd like to talk to you about a situation that has been bothering me. I need your help in figuring out how to resolve the problem."

You can help your child by listening carefully to him when he does bring up an issue with you. By hearing what he has to say, you are telling him that it is okay to directly bring up issues with you.

| Step Six | *Watch body language.* |

You can tell a lot about what people feel by watching their body language. Are they sitting with arms, legs, and fingers crossed, and a scowl on their face? Those are not good signs for open communication. Shelve the discussion until their body posture appears more relaxed and open.

Be aware of your own body language. If you notice your own body language is communicating tension, anger, or hostility, let your child know. "This is not a good time for me to talk about this. I'm feeling too cranky. Let's talk again after dinner."

| Step Seven | *Restate the feelings of the other person.* |

This lets the other person know they are being heard and are worth listening to. "What I hear you saying is that you are frustrated because I asked you to do your homework as soon as you got home, and you would like a snack first. Is that correct?"

Practice the Reflective Listening game in Chapter Three of this book. This game will help your child restate the feelings of the other person in an argument. Practice this game whenever conflicts arise. Ask your child to tell you how he thinks you're feeling when he's in conflict with you. Children tend to forget that their parents also have their own feelings during a heated discussion.

Step Eight	*Come to the table with compromises in mind.*

In your preplanning stage, you can already have in mind several actions you can take to resolve the situation. Make sure these are changes that you, yourself, can make. If you come to the table with changes only the other person can make, you won't be successful. If you show the other person that you are willing to make changes, he is more likely to do the same.

Compromising with your child is not the same thing as allowing your child to control the interaction and dictate its ending. Give your child some choices, but maintain your expectations. For instance, "Bobby, you are in too many after-school activities. You may choose two out of the three activities, but you need to drop one." Bobby may say he doesn't want to drop any of them, but that's not an option. You are giving him the choice of which activity he wants to drop. You are not giving him the option to continue to do all three.

Step Nine | *Stick to "I feel..." statements.*

When you say, "I feel . . ." rather than "You did . . ." or "You are a . . .", you are more likely to get cooperation and less likely to make someone defensive. Read the following statements. Which sounds better to you?

> "You are such a slob. It makes me crazy."

> or

> "I feel taken advantage of when I see your room is a mess, especially since I've told you to straighten it up."

Help your child express his feelings with words, not actions. When you hear your child appropriately let someone know how he feels, praise him for his efforts.

Step Ten | *See your own role in a problem.*

This is especially important when you are arguing with your child. If you demonstrate for your child that you are ready to change your own behavior in order to solve a problem, your child is more likely to take responsibility for his own actions, and work with you toward a mutually agreeable solution.

Resolving Conflicts Calmly

During a conflict, it's essential that your child maintain control of himself. Many children, as well as adults, have an automatic stress response to conflict—they become angry, upset, and excited. Situations can easily blow up and get out of hand. When you see your child getting upset, help him learn to change his automatic stress response to a calm, cool, and collected one. The following guidelines will help.

Tips For Resolving Conflicts Calmly

▸ Make a positive statement. "I can handle this situation."

▸ Put the situation in perspective. "This is not that big a deal. No problem!"

▸ Use humor to diffuse the situation.

▸ Focus first on the other person's perspective. "I'm going to try to understand where this person is coming from before I get upset."

▸ Don't sweat the small stuff.

▸ Ask for help from positive people. Stay away from people you know are going to make you angry.

▸ Take a deep breath.

▸ Postpone dealing with it. "I'm going to wait until I calm down before I try to handle this situation."

▸ Distract yourself. "I'm going to focus on my schoolwork right now until I feel myself calming down."

▸ Get a good night's sleep. "I'm always more cranky when I haven't slept enough. I'm going to sleep on this problem and deal with it in the morning."

▸ Take some time to think about an issue before you react.

▸ Delay your automatic reaction. Even a few minutes of waiting before reacting can mean the difference between having a calm, rather than a heated, discussion.

Charlie and His Dad— A Successful Resolution

Let's revisit the situation between Charlie and his dad that began this chapter. This time around, Dad decides to approach the situation differently. He already knows from previous experience that Charlie will try to procrastinate on cleaning his room, but Dad has planned ahead and developed potential compromises. Dad goes into the conversation calmer and cooler. He has decided he is not going to let Charlie make him angry, and he will not allow himself to resort to poor conflict resolution behavior. Here is how the dialogue goes:

(Charlie is playing Nintendo.)

Dad: "Charlie, your room is messy. It needs to be picked up."

Charlie: "I will. In a minute, Dad."

Dad: "I see that you are in the middle of a game. And I also know how long the games can last. I'm going to set the timer for ten minutes. When the bell rings, it's time to clean your room. Is that a deal?"

Charlie: "Sure, Dad."

(Five minutes pass.)

Dad: "Charlie, you have five minutes until you have to clean your room."

Charlie: "Yup."

(Three more minutes pass.)

Dad: "Charlie, two more minutes."

Charlie: "I'm almost done."

(One minute passes.)

Dad: "One more minute, and then I shut off the Nintendo."

(One minute passes.)
(Dad calmly shuts off the Nintendo.)

Charlie: *(Whining)* "Daaaad! I was almost at the end of the game!"

Dad: *(Being direct in what he needs and restating Charlie's feelings)* "I know it's hard to break away from your game, but I gave you ample time. I need you to clean up your room now."

Charlie: *(Walking into his bedroom)* "I don't want to now. I only had one more minute left on the game."

Dad: *(Still calm)* "The clothes need to be put away. The bed needs to be made. The desk needs to be straightened. Then you can go back to your Nintendo."

Charlie: "Aw, Dad!"

Dad: "The sooner you get it done, the sooner you can get back to your game. I know you can do it." *(Dad leaves the room and goes downstairs.)*

(Charlie complains and whines a little longer, but he does pick up the room.)

(Later)

Dad: "It makes me feel good that you did such a good job cleaning your room. How did you do on the game? Did you get to the next level?"

If you noticed, this time Dad did not resort to lecturing or labeling Charlie's behavior. He maintained his expectations, allowed Charlie some leeway to play a bit longer, but then stuck to the limit he initially set. He also allowed Charlie to gripe a little without giving in to him. The conflict was resolved successfully!

Conflict Resolution Games and Exercises

1. The Do's and Don'ts of Conflict Resolution

Review the following checklist of Do's and Don'ts. Pay special attention to the Don'ts, all of which will almost guarantee an unsuccessful resolution to the conflict.

Do's:	Don'ts:
▸ Treat the other person with respect throughout the conversation.	▸ Don't use threats.
▸ Try to understand the other person's position.	▸ Don't use putdowns or insults.
▸ Acknowledge the feelings of the other person.	▸ Don't yell or cuss.
▸ Restate the other person's feelings.	▸ Don't make commands.
▸ Give the other person a chance to express himself.	▸ Don't interrupt.
▸ State your needs calmly and directly.	▸ Don't be sarcastic.
▸ Compromise.	▸ Don't exaggerate.
▸ Use positive body language.	▸ Don't speak for another person.
▸ Have a good sense of humor.	▸ Don't lecture.
▸ Attack the problem, not the person.	▸ Don't arouse guilt.

2. The Family Meeting

Family meetings are a wonderful way to help your child learn conflict resolution skills.

▸ Choose a consistent time each week to have a meeting. Many families choose Friday or Sunday evenings.

▸ At the meeting, have each person say one positive thing about each family member.

▸ After positive statements have been shared, allow each person a chance to share a gripe about one family member.

▸ Help your child phrase gripes in "I feel . . . " language.

▸ Help the person who is being griped about restate the feelings.

▸ When someone complains about you, make sure you model good conflict resolution behavior.

▸ Brainstorm solutions to each problem.

▸ Choose a plan of action for dealing with each problem.

▸ Follow through on the plan.

3. The Pretend Argument

Stage a pretend argument with your child. Role-play the argument. Give points for using good conflict resolution techniques.

Chapter Ten

MANAGING ANGER

Putting It All Together

Managing Anger

Resolving Conflicts

Solving Social Problems

Managing Stress

Coping with Teasing

Raising Self-Esteem

Reading Social Signals

Communicating and Conversing

Joining In

Getting Started

GOALS ▸

In this chapter, you will learn how to help your child:

- ✓ Understand what "pushes his buttons."
- ✓ Recognize how his body expresses anger.
- ✓ Appreciate anger as a "normal" emotion.
- ✓ Find healthy ways to express anger.
- ✓ Master "positive self-talk."
- ✓ Decrease aggressive behavior.
- ✓ Use "I feel . . . " statements.
- ✓ Find physical outlets for angry feelings.
- ✓ Keep an anger control log.

Jimmy

*J**immy's parents can always tell when he's getting ready to blow up because his face turns red, he grits his teeth, and he clenches his fists. Jimmy loses control when he is angry. He throws things and breaks them, yells insults and threats, and even hits whomever is nearby at the time. After he calms down, Jimmy feels guilty about his outburst and promises his parents that he will never behave like that again. But inevitably, Jimmy becomes angry and loses control again. He regularly gets angry when he loses at a game or when he really wants something that his parents won't let him have. Jimmy's parents don't know how to help their son handle his anger more effectively and less aggressively.*

Claire

C *laire keeps things bottled up inside of her. She rarely expresses anger. Instead, she allows people to insult her and mistreat her, and she never mentions a word about it. Her parents would never know that anything is bothering her, except that every once in a while, Claire will overreact to a minor offense. Seemingly out of the blue, she will become very upset and tearful about a small matter, such as a friend forgetting to call her or her mother giving her food she doesn't like. Claire's dad also keeps his emotions hidden. He bottles up everything inside, and then occasionally blows his top by yelling and screaming. Claire's mother, on the other hand, rarely expresses anger, but is prone to bouts of sadness and depression when things are bothering her. Both Claire and her parents could use help expressing their angry feelings in a healthy fashion.*

Anger management is often one of the primary concerns for parents because the inability to manage anger effectively is very disruptive to family life. Managing anger is also one of the most challenging social skills for a child to learn because it requires him to build on other social skills (such as those addressed in previous chapters). For instance, unless a child is able to resolve conflicts using good social skills, his conflicts will escalate into angry battles. And, if a child improves at reading social signals, his interactions are less likely to build into occasions for anger. Because this is such a challenging social skill to master, we have saved it for last.

The Anger Control Quiz

Ask yourself the following questions to determine if your child might need help learning how to manage his anger more appropriately:

☐ Does your child become angry quickly?

☐ Do minor troubles tend to annoy your child more than they do most children?

☐ Does your child get into a lot of arguments with others?

☐ Does your child get into fistfights with other children?

☐ Does your child become very upset when things don't go his way?

☐ Does your child tend to store up anger until he explodes?

☐ Does your child yell and scream when he is angry?

☐ Does your child cry uncontrollably when he is angry?

☐ Does your child throw and/or break things when he is angry?

☐ Does your child's anger affect his academic performance?

If you answered *yes* to any of the above questions, your child may be having trouble controlling and expressing his anger in a healthy way. You can learn ways to help your child "keep his cool" and stay in control.

Anger is a Natural Emotion

Anger is a normal, healthy emotion that all human beings feel from time to time. It actually can be a helpful emotion because it lets us know that something is wrong and needs to change. As your child begins to feel more comfortable with anger and how to express it in a controlled fashion, he will appreciate how anger helps him.

Anger only becomes problematic when there is too much of it, or it is expressed in either an uncontrolled or an overcontrolled manner. In the above examples, Jimmy's anger is uncontrolled while Claire's anger is overcontrolled. When anger is not

> **Anger Helps Us:**
> ▸ reach goals
> ▸ stay healthy
> ▸ work through problems
> ▸ feel better about ourselves
> ▸ understand ourselves better
> ▸ be clearer with others about our needs

expressed appropriately, it can lead to tensions at home, difficulties at school, physical and mental problems, and relationship conflicts. The first step in controlling anger is understanding its roots and how the body exhibits it. Then we can move on to helping your child learn to express anger appropriately.

Step One *Understand anger.*

First and foremost, children need to know that anger is an acceptable emotion to feel. But they need to learn the

difference between feeling and action. The feeling is okay, but acting on anger without self-control is NOT okay. Talk to your child about anger. Explain to him that anger is a normal emotion. Ask your child why he thinks expressing anger appropriately would be important.

Jimmy and Claire's parents would start by first discussing with their children why it's so important to release anger in a healthy way. Jimmy's parents would begin by asking their son, "Why is it not okay to lose your self-control when you are angry?" Jimmy's answers could be written down and posted somewhere private where Jimmy could review them periodically. Here is a sample list:

1. If I lose control, I lose friends.

2. If I lose control, I get in trouble at school and at home.

3. If I lose control, I feel badly about myself.

4. If I lose control, I feel unhappy.

5. If I lose control, I might hurt someone.

6. If I lose control, I might say hurtful things I regret.

Claire's parents would begin by asking their daughter, "What happens if you keep your anger inside for a long time without letting anyone know?" Here is Claire's sample list:

1. If I store up my anger, I will feel sad inside.
2. If I store up my anger, I might explode later.
3. If I store up my anger, I might make myself sick.
4. If I store up my anger, I can't get what I need.
5. If I store up my anger, it's hard for others to understand how I feel.

Step Two | **_Help your child discover what "pushes his buttons" (makes him mad)._**

Most children are quite clear about what makes them angry. As a matter of fact, children identify anger as the prime emotion they feel when things do not go their way. The first step in gaining control over anger is knowing ahead of time what "pushes your buttons." Once your child knows this about himself, he is more able to:

▸ Avoid situations that will anger him

Avoid Situations that Make You Mad

THERE'S BECKY. SHE IS ALWAYS MEAN To ME... I'M GOING TO WALK ON THE OTHER SIDE OF THE STREET So SHE DOESN'T SEE ME.

▶ Come up with solutions to his anger ahead of time

▶ Soothe himself when confronted with an anger-producing situation

Sit down with your child and brainstorm about the different kinds of situations that make him angry—his personal "button pushers." Write down every idea that your child comes up with. Here is a sample list:

Button Pushers

▶ Not getting what I want

▶ Being teased

▶ Getting yelled at

▶ Stressful homework assignments

▶ Losing a game

▶ Being bugged by my sister or brother

▶ When I feel ignored or unloved

▶ When things aren't fair

▶ When I get bossed around

After your child comes up with his list, emphasize to your child how important it is to be aware of what gets him mad so that he can begin to control his anger.

Step Three	*Recognize the warning signs of anger.*

It's especially difficult for children to calm themselves down once they begin to feel the signs of anger. It can be helpful if you are aware of your own child's warning signs so that you can intervene BEFORE he entirely loses control. Help your child to identify his body's anger warning signals.

Ask your child to notice the physical warning signs that he exhibits when he becomes angry. Here is a sample list:

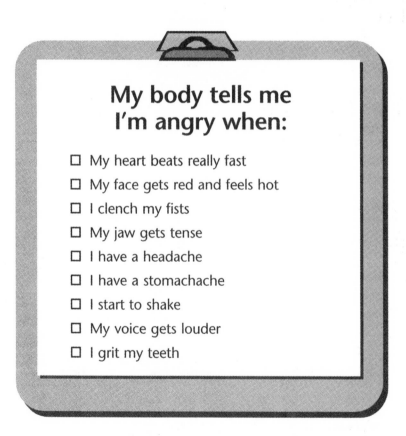

My body tells me I'm angry when:

☐ My heart beats really fast
☐ My face gets red and feels hot
☐ I clench my fists
☐ My jaw gets tense
☐ I have a headache
☐ I have a stomachache
☐ I start to shake
☐ My voice gets louder
☐ I grit my teeth

Once both you and your child know your child's specific body signs, then you both can team up when he is angry to get the anger under control. In Jimmy's situation, his parents know that when Jimmy gets angry his face gets red and he clenches his fists and teeth. When they see these signs, his parents can say to him, "Jimmy, you're showing anger signs, why don't you go to your room and cool off?" or "Jimmy, your body is saying you are angry, why don't you go through the steps to control anger that we've talked about?" Claire's parents can say, "Claire, I see that your face looks upset, can you let us know how you are feeling?" or "Claire, your body tells us that you are angry, can you put it into words?"

Step Four | ***Express anger appropriately.***

Now that your child has a better idea of what makes him angry, you can discuss ways to help him express it appropriately. He has learned what his body feels like when he's angry. He has also learned from the conflict resolution chapter that yelling, blaming, labeling, and insulting are not appropriate ways to resolve arguments or express anger. And he has seen from Claire's example that keeping anger bottled up is not healthy either. "Anger bottlers" run the risk of having health problems or angry outbursts in the future.

Anger Control
Games and Exercises

The following exercises will help your child strengthen his "anger control" muscles:

1. Anger Tracking

Track anger in the family. It's critical that parents be aware of their own methods for expressing anger. By tracking anger in the house, you can identify family members that express anger similarly. Parents who struggle with their own inappropriate expressions of anger can then work on getting themselves under control first. Modeling good anger control is key to helping your child gain control.

Track anger outbursts in the family. Count how many times per week each child and parent has an angry outburst.

	Child	Child	Parent	Parent
Monday				
Tuesday				
Wednesday				
Thursday				
Friday				
Saturday				
Sunday				

In addition, track how your family's anger is expressed. Mark the behaviors you witnessed.

	Child	Child	Parent	Parent
Crying/Tears				
Yelling/Shouting				
Throwing things				
Slamming doors				
Hitting				
Leaving the room				
Speaking directly				
Other				

2. Draw It

Ask your child to draw on a piece of paper three acceptable things he can do with his angry feelings (for example, practicing relaxation, hitting a pillow, and so on.)

3. Role-Play

Start by demonstrating for your child how you would express anger in a particular situation. Then allow your child to give you feedback on how you did. Next, let your child role-play a situation, expressing anger in a healthy way.

Here's an example: "Every day at school, a girl named Amanda pulls kids aside and whispers behind my back. This makes me very angry. How can I handle my anger?"

Mom role-plays first.

Mom: "Amanda, I feel hurt when you whisper behind my back. What exactly are you whispering about?"

Amanda: "What are you talking about? I'm not whispering about you."

Mom: "Oh, I'm sorry. In that case, you won't mind if I join you in this conversation then."

Your child gives feedback.

Child: "That was really good, Mom. I'm going to try that."

Mom: "Why don't you try it right now?"

Child role-plays next, practicing what Mom has modeled.

4. Handling Anger Quiz

Give your child the following quiz to see if he can tell the difference between appropriate and inappropriate responses to anger.

Situation: A teacher accuses you of cheating. You did not cheat. Review the following possible responses and mark the ones that are appropriate ways to deal with this situation.

Check Appropriate Responses:

☐ Yell at the teacher.

☐ Threaten to tell the principal about the teacher.

☐ Become very upset by crying.

☐ Ignore the teacher by walking away.

☐ Agree with the teacher.

☐ Tell the teacher calmly that you did not cheat.

☐ Offer to take the test again.

5. Keep a weekly anger control journal.

Help your child track his anger and his responses to his anger to see if he is gaining more control.

Date: _____

Describe the situation that got you mad.

_____

_____

Describe how your body felt when you got mad.

_____

_____

Did you think about ways to express your anger?

_____

_____

Did you think about the consequences to these actions?

_____

_____

Which coping techniques did you use?

_____

_____

Were you successful in expressing anger the way you hoped? *(circle one)*

Not at all   A little bit   Pretty much   Yes, very!!

Signature of Child _____

Signature of Parent _____

6. Change negative thoughts to positive ones.

Ask your child to choose a recent situation that has bothered him. Have him fill out the following worksheet. Review with him how important it is to think positively, because positive thoughts create positive feelings.

1. Describe the situation.

_____

_____

_____

2. Describe my negative thoughts about the situation.

_____

_____

_____

3. What are positive ways I can think about the situation?

_____

_____

_____

4. What is my new way of seeing the situation?

_____

_____

_____

5. What are my feelings now?

_____

_____

_____

7. Write "Do" thoughts and post them.

Help your child write a list of "Do" thoughts he can think to himself when things upset him. Post them in key places around the house, such as on the refrigerator, on his bedroom door, and so on.

Sample "Do" Thoughts List:

I'm thinking about something else.

I'm calm.

Maybe this was just an accident.

I'm keeping my distance.

I can handle it.

I'm staying cool.

This is no big deal.

I'm relaxed.

I'm taking a deep breath.

8. Practice "I feel . . ." statements.

Have your child change the following "blame" statements into "I feel . . ." statements. This exercise is harder than it looks.

"You're always late, and it drives me crazy!"

Instead,

"I feel _____ when you _____.
Next time, I would like it if you would_____."

"You are such a jerk!"

Instead,

"I feel _____ when you _____.
Next time, I would like it if you would_____."

"You are so annoying!"

Instead,

"I feel _____ when you _____ .
Next time, I would like it if you would _____."

"(Choose your own blame statement)"

Instead,

"I feel _____ when you _____ .
Next time, I would like it if you would _____."

9. Set an anger-control management plan.

Gaining control of anger is a gradual process. You will need to set goals, track progress, and reward your child for steps in the right direction. It's tempting to reward only perfection. But remember, there is no perfection in the realm of anger control, so reward each baby step toward the goal!

Goal	Target Date	Completion Date	Reward
Sample: I will have fewer than five temper outbursts this week	9/20	9/20	Ice cream for dessert

Chapter Eleven

PUTTING IT
ALL TOGETHER

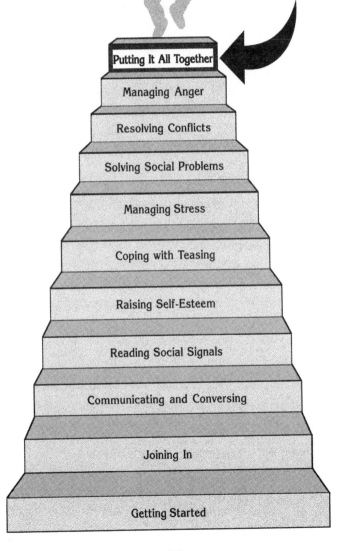

Putting It All Together

Managing Anger

Resolving Conflicts

Solving Social Problems

Managing Stress

Coping with Teasing

Raising Self-Esteem

Reading Social Signals

Communicating and Conversing

Joining In

Getting Started

Conclusion

Congratulations! You and your child have completed the stepping stones necessary to build people skills. Remember that raising your child's social IQ is no simple task. You may find that even after reading the entire book, practicing the exercises recommended, and reviewing lessons learned, your child still struggles with basic social skills. Don't be discouraged. It may take a long time for your child to acquire new skills. You may want to revisit certain chapters that were challenging for your child. I encourage you to spend as much time as is necessary for your child to begin to comfortably use his new skills in real-life situations. Like any new skill, practice is going to make all the difference. The more you can incorporate social skills practice into your child's daily life, the more proficient your child will be at using these skills.

Some children do need more individualized attention. If you are still frustrated with your child's progress, there are other options you can pursue. First, consult with your school's guidance counselor. Many schools conduct social skills groups to help children develop positive social behaviors. However, there are both advantages and disadvantages to school programs. One advantage is that usually there is no fee for these groups. Another advantage is that the groups take place at school, requiring no additional time commitment in your schedule. The school groups also contain children with whom your child can develop friendships. The disadvantages to these groups are that they tend to be time-limited (usually meeting for no more than 12 weeks) and brief. Some groups take place during lunch, which is usually only half an hour long. This can make it challenging to apply skills from group to real-life situations. Another disadvantage is that often parents are not actively involved in the process, and thus are not able to offer the support and practice that outside groups offer.

A school group, however, can work nicely in combination with an outside therapy group. Programs like Stepping Stones are cropping up around the country. In evaluating possible programs, keep the following in mind:

1. Research the program thoroughly.

Make sure the program is well-established. Talk to graduates of the program. Find out the specifics of how each group is structured. Is the program centered on the development of specific skills? For social skills training, it is useful to know the specific skills practiced and how the skills are taught.

2. Find out the level of expertise of the group leaders.

Many insurance companies will cover group therapy under their mental health coverage. However, they will cover only those who are licensed within their particular profession. For instance, licensed clinical social workers and licensed clinical psychologists are covered by most insurance plans. It is perfectly appropriate for you to ask how many years the group leaders have been practicing, and how long they have been running groups.

There are many well-qualified therapists who have been practicing for many years, but have little group therapy experience. Group therapy is a very different type of treatment and requires a special kind of expertise.

3. Choose a group program that includes parents so that you and your child can practice skills in between sessions.

This requires a large commitment on your part. It certainly would be easier to drop off your child each week to be "fixed," but in my experience, parental participation means the difference between skills that transfer from one environment to another and skills that don't. It's worth it for you to put in the effort to get the most out of the program.

> ▸ Research the program thoroughly.
> ▸ Find out the experience level of the people leading the groups.
> ▸ Choose one that includes parents so that you and your child can practice skills in between sessions.

4. Choose a program that is more than just a few weeks long.

Some programs offer 6–12 week sessions. You may feel that you will save money, time, and energy by enrolling in one of these programs. The problem is that these short-term programs are not effective. It is unrealistic to expect your child to learn skills and be able to perform them in different situations in only a few short weeks.

The transfer of social skills from a group program to home and school can be difficult, but it's certainly not impossible. With the right combination of program, practice, and support from you, your child can raise his social IQ and feel less alone, more connected to other kids, and happy in his life.

Afterword

For parents of children with special needs

Although Stepping Stones, the social skills training program outlined in this book, is designed to help any child with social concerns, these techniques are also appropriate and can be geared specifically to children with more serious interpersonal challenges—for example, children diagnosed with Attention Deficit/Hyperactivity Disorder (AD/HD), Asperger's Syndrome or High Functioning Autism (HFA), or children diagnosed with Nonverbal Learning Disabilities (NLD).

If your child has special challenges, you may want to engage a therapist in your area who specializes in social skills training with children, in addition to working with your child on social skill development at home. A trained psychotherapist can help you develop realistic expectations so that you and your child don't become discouraged or feel overwhelmed. New social skills can be difficult for any child to master, and it's important that you introduce these concepts to your child in a way that is both empowering and realistic.

Experts in the field of social skills training are well aware of the need to break goals down into small, achievable increments so that your child can accomplish them successfully. In addition, the experienced group leader uses structure and dynamics to reinforce agreed upon goals. The group becomes a microcosm for the social arena at school or in the neighborhood. Group members act as mentors for each other. They practice skills together through role play, give each other positive feedback and constructive criticism, and gain strength from knowing that they are not alone with their social struggles.

If you are unable to find a good social skills training program in your local area, parents are encouraged to become their child's social skills coach. You can help your child by setting achievable goals, modeling and rehearsing newly developing skills, and reinforcing those that have been mastered. Involve siblings, when possible, as this relationship can be a safe interpersonal ground to resolve conflicts, practice problem-solving, and try new anger control methods.

Considerations for parents of children with AD/HD

Not all children with AD/HD have social skills problems. And social challenges can vary depending upon the age of the child, the type of AD/HD, and the sex of the child. In addition to reading this book, parents of children with AD/HD should educate themselves about the impact of AD/HD by reading several of the numerous books that focus exclusively on AD/HD. Please refer to the bibliography at the end of this chapter.

The child with AD/HD generally exhibits a constellation of characteristics that may interfere with successful social skill development:

1. The emotions of children with AD/HD tend to be extreme, poorly modulated, and subject to rapid fluctuations.

Because of this heightened emotional picture, the child with AD/HD is seen as unpredictable by peers. This may lead to bullying by peers who view him or her as someone whose buttons are easily pushed. The aggressor relishes "getting a rise" out of an emotionally volatile child. A child's tendency towards low frustration tolerance due to AD/HD only serves to exacerbate his emotional outbursts.

2. The child with AD/HD may be insensitive to subtle interpersonal cues.

Being able to recognize and understand the body language and facial expressions of others requires children to regularly scan their environment for clues that will guide their social actions. Because children with AD/HD often struggle to stay tuned in to their environments, social signals are misread. There are several social issues that may result from this misunderstanding of social signals from peers. Misinterpretation can lead to overreacting to ambiguous social situations. It can also lead to "under reaction". The child who does not see the signals may be insensitive to the feedback cues, i.e. facial expressions, body language of others, leading to frustration and anger from peers who feel that their "social hints" are being disregarded.

3. The child with AD/HD may be impulsive.

When a child lacks the adequate pause between impulse and action, social "faux pas" inevitably occur. Poor listening skills are a common byproduct of impulsivity. When a child is unable to pause before speaking or acting, he or she also struggles to screen out inappropriate thoughts that may hurt others' feelings. When conversations don't have a natural "give and take" because of these struggles, peers become turned off because they feel unheard.

4. The chronic stress of the daily struggle of school may lead to low self-esteem.

A child with high self-esteem has much better chances of making appropriate social choices than the child with low self-esteem. Children with low self-esteem may be prone to depression. Some even become shy and reclusive, walling themselves off from peers altogether. The socially neglected child, the one who walks unseen down the corridor at school, is going to experience as much social pain as the socially rejected.

5. Children with AD/HD have a very hard time learning from experience, whether that experience is positive or negative.

In other words, when a non-AD/HD child makes a social mistake and receives a hostile reaction from his peers, chances are high that he will not make that same mistake again. The child with AD/HD, on the other hand, may make the mistake repeatedly before he or she learns not to do it again. By this time, potential friends are too irritated to be accepting.

6. Children with AD/HD may not respond to reward or punishment as predictably.

For instance, if a child with AD/HD offers to help a classmate with a project, and the classmate is grateful and returns the favor, he or she might not recognize that they were rewarded for appropriate behavior. As a result, the child with AD/HD may do something antisocial the next time the opportunity to help arises. This unpredictable behavior confuses peers.

7. Children with AD/HD may have a difficult time predicting audience response.

A non-AD/HD child may realize that others will view his own strange behavior as "weird." This knowledge informs his behavior. Children with AD/HD get themselves into social binds without being aware of their predicament or of how they got there because they lack awareness of the consequences of their social behavior.

It is important to make a distinction here between the social worlds of girls and boys. Boys and girls tend to interact in same-sex groups. They also play very differently from each other. Boys' play tends to involve physical, roughhousing and athletic endeavors; girls' play tends to focus on forming friendships and developing intimacies. Because of these very basic differences between boys and girls, girls are generally even more sensitive to social rejection and neglect than boys.

For the child with AD/HD, the above mentioned characteristics may be common in both sexes but they surface and get played out quite differently between boys and girls. In addition, male and female peers react to these characteristics disparately as well. Generally, there is a bit more social rope given to boys than to girls. After all, the "boys will be boys" philosophy espouses that boys are impulsive by nature. Society may turn a blind eye to boys that resolve differences through fighting, for instance. Blurting out by boys as well as verbal sparring is quite common, perhaps even condoned, lending some protection to the impulsive boy with AD/HD. When a boy with AD/HD is very athletic, physically powerful, for instance, he may be able to compensate for his social weaknesses with his physical strengths.

Girls, on the other hand, are generally socialized to be a part of their peer group. Physical prowess is not deemed as important; social savvy is highly stressed, thus the unique social challenges of girls with AD/HD are met with more rigidity and rejection than that of their male counterpart. If a girl stands out in a negative way from her peers, especially when these ways are not in keeping with sex role stereotypes, she will most certainly be excluded, if not down right rejected by her female peers. Less leeway is given to the verbally or physically impulsive girl with AD/HD.

Once your child has earned a negative social reputation, it is quite difficult to help him undo the damage. It can be accomplished, but the work is slow. It is up to you, as the parent, to understand fully what may have contributed to your child's poor social reputation. This alone can be a very heartbreaking chore. No parent wants to see that their child's behavior may be contributing to their social standing. Unfortunately, no change can take place until you can fully appreciate the behaviors your child exhibits that turn other children off.

What can a parent of a child with AD/HD do?

1. Make sure your child has been properly evaluated and is being actively treated for his or her AD/HD, i.e. medication management, social skills training, behavior management, etc.

The AD/HD literature stresses the need for a multidimensional approach to treatment. Make sure all of your helping professionals coordinate their treatment strategies and goals.

2. Keep in close contact with your child's teacher(s).

Ask teachers to reinforce goals and practice learned skills with all of their students. Ask teachers to help you get a clear picture of your child's social functioning at school.

3. Observe your child carefully to see which behaviors are alienating peers.

4. Develop "self-monitoring" opportunities for your child.

You must stress the importance to your child of developing his ability to see the way others see him or her.

5. Encourage your child to keep a low profile at school and in the neighborhood until more effective social skills have developed.

6. Begin to set circumscribed goals to work on with your child with AD/HD that will address his or her social deficits.

7. Only encourage play activities with peers that know and appreciate your child.

This is not the time to expose your child to new friends. This will only serve to reinforce negative reputations as skills have not developed yet.

8. Decline invitations that will set your child up for a social disaster, i.e. a sleep-over or large party.

You don't want to burn bridges in the process of protecting your child from disasters. Politely decline but leave the door open for future play experiences and invitations.

9. Choose play activities that are intrinsically simple for your child in terms of attention span and stimulation.

Keep the activities as short as your child needs. If he or she can't play for more than an hour with another child, keep the play date short.

10. Encourage friendships with non-AD/HD peers who have mellow temperaments.

Although children with AD/HD are attracted to the energy and excitement of other children with AD/HD, discourage these friendships because two children with AD/HD are even more difficult to guide than one.

11. Play the role of supportive guide.

You may need to be more present during your child's social commitment, but this does not mean you need to be there to supervise and control the interaction every step of the way. This is a difficult high-wire act for many parents.

AD/HD Resources

Quinn, P. and Stern, J. *Putting on the Brakes.* Washington, DC: American Psychological Association Press, 2008 (second edition). *A top-selling classic for elementary school aged kids.*

Nadeau, K. and Dixon, E. *Learing to Slow Down and Pay Attention.* Washington, DC: American Psychological Association Press, 1997. *Appealing, cartoon-illustrated, with lots of practical, kid-friendly tips.*

Roberts, B. *The Adventures of Phoebe Flower.* (4-part reading series). Washington, DC: Advantage Books, 1998, 1999, 2000, 2002. *A charming series of books for kids ages 8-11 depicting a very positive, but realistic image of a young girl with ADHD.*

Quinn, P. and Stern, J. *The "Putting on the Brakes" Activity Book for Young People with ADHD.* Washington, DC: American Psychological Association, 2009 (second edition).

Nadeau, K., Littman, E., & Quinn, P. *Understanding Girls with ADHD.* Washington, DC: Advantage Books, 1999. *A guide for parents of girls from preschool through high school that focuses on social skills issues at every age, as well as on a broad range of other ADHD-related concerns.*

Quinn, P. *Attention, Girls! A Guide to Learn about Your ADHD.* Washington, DC: Magination Press, 2009. *Meet other girls just like you and learn lots of ways to take charge of ADHD.*

Considerations for parents of children with Nonverbal Learning Disabilities (NLD)

The syndrome of nonverbal learning disabilities (NLD) has also recently become a distinct diagnostic entity with its own specific social repercussions. Because much of social communication is nonverbal, involving body language, facial expressions, and tone of voice, children with NLD are at a significant social disadvantage. They tend to miss important signals in social interaction and almost always fail to appreciate nuances in behavior. When an NLD child misunderstands affective intonation, verbal feedback is frequently misunderstood. All of the above can lead to significant weaknesses in social perception, including social judgment and social problem-solving. Another major characteristic of NLD children is a lack of adaptability. The ability to deal with change is a fundamental aspect of social competency. Because of these interpersonal challenges, NLD children may struggle to form intimate relationships. This, in turn, can contribute to feelings of low self-worth.

What can a parent of a child with NLD do?

1. The most effective plan for intervention with a child with NLD is to first get your child accurately diagnosed.

This almost always necessitates a thorough neuropsychological evaluation. Once a proper diagnosis has been achieved, a plan for intervention can follow that focuses on compensating for deficits and building on strengths.

2. Practical daily activities need to be taught.

It is not uncommon for a child with NLD to struggle with skills that require nonverbal or math skills, i.e. chores, organizing materials. Compensatory mechanisms are helpful, i.e. post-it notes™, clear boxes for toys, open shelves, using a tape recorder during class.

3. Because children with NLD have trouble mentally "picturing" information, they may not be able to visualize consequences.

Help your child come up with alternative solutions to problems and then role play solutions that are productive and accurate.

4. Practice a skill set over and over.

Children with NLD, with repeated practice, are able to develop social proficiencies. It is important that you are willing to break the skills down into manageable increments.

5. Review and practice language commonly used on a daily basis.

Help your child with NLD understand and use common phrases such as "hello," "how are you?" "I'm fine," etc.

6. Ask your child to repeat a neutral phrase within different emotional contexts.

For instance, ask your child to say, "I want to play" as if they are angry, sad, happy, or excited. Likewise, you can repeat the neutral phrase with differing emotions and ask your child to guess what you are feeling.

NLD References

Rourke, B.P. *Nonverbal learning disabilities: The syndrome and the model.* New York: Guilford Press, 1989.

Rourke, B.P. *Syndrome of nonverbal learning disabilities: Neurodevelopmental manifestations.* New York: Guilford Press, 1995.

For the parents of the child with Asperger's Syndrome or High-functioning Autism

In the last few decades, the child diagnosed with Asperger's Syndrome has literally exploded into our consciousness. These children, sometimes referred to as children with High-functioning Autism, lack social skills, have a limited ability to have a reciprocal conversation, and demonstrate an intense absorption in certain limited subjects (which may or may not be of interest to anyone else beside themselves). Seemingly unaware of the unwritten rules of social conduct, children with Asperger's inadvertently offend peers by saying and doing things that are insensitive to peers' feelings. They have few genuine friends and seem virtually unable to read people's body language. Parents of these children describe their children as being socially isolated at best and may even be socially abused and rejected by peers.

Children with Asperger's do not learn the way other children learn. They may find complex computer operations a breeze to figure out but are terribly confused by the most simple verbal or nonverbal communications. Despite the disruptions these children have in their social learning, social skills training using cognitive-behavioral methods are effective in helping them to improve their relationships with peers. The child with Asperger's can gradually learn the codes of social conduct, more through intellectual analysis and instruction than natural intuition. The process outlined in this book is developmentally sequenced so that easier concepts and skills are taught and complex skills are not introduced until the child has mastered the previous skill set. It is very important to build upon a child's successes and expand upon them.

What can a parent of a child with Asperger's do?

1. Familiarize yourself with the social games and activities being played by children of a similar age as your child.

Practice these popular games. For instance, if playing with balls is a common activity, enlist your child in several minutes a day of ball playing.

2. Go over the rules of play with your child.

Be aware that sometimes the most basic rules of play have to be explained. For instance, you may feel that it is obvious that you only kick the ball into your own goal, but your child may not understand this concept automatically.

3. Give other options besides "stating the obvious".

The child with Asperger's may say "I don't like you and don't want to play with you". You may have to teach him other options for expressing his feelings such as, "I want to play by myself right now".

4. Encourage taking the other child's perspective.

Rarely does a child with Asperger's intend to hurt another child's feelings. You may need to help him understand the impact he has on others. And, consistently ask him to explain how the other person may have felt as a consequence of what he said or did.

5. Expose your child to natural play environments.

Insure the occasion is a success by encouraging play situations which minimize the influence of the child's limited social play skills.

6. Enroll the child in clubs.

The advantage of these activities is that they are usually supervised and structured.

7. Ask your child to look at what other children are doing.

Let your child know that, as long as others are behaving appropriately, they can be good role models for modes of social conduct.

8. Use this book flexibly.

Although the chapters in this book are sequenced from simple to more complex, there is no need to rigidly adhere to following it in a step-by-step fashion. Evaluate your child's unique strengths and weaknesses and develop a program that meets those unique needs.

Asperger's Resources

Attwood, Tony. Asperger's Syndrome: *A Guide for Parents and Professionals.* London: Jessica Kingsley Publishers, 1997.

Cohen, Shirley. *Targeting Autism: What We Know, Don't Know, and Can Do to Help Young Children with Autism and Related Disorders.* Berkeley, CA: University of California Press, 1998.

Fling, Echo R. *Eating an Artichoke: A Mother's Perspective on Asperger Syndrome.* London: Jessica Kingsley Publishers, 2000.

Gray, C.A. (in press) *'Social stories and comic strip conversations with students with Asperger Syndrome and high functioning autism.'* In E. Schopler, G.B. Mesibov and L. Kunce (Eds.) Asperger's Syndrome and High Functioning Autism. New York: Plenum Press.

Myles, Brenda Smith, & Southwick, Jack. *Asperger's Syndrome and Difficult Moments: Practical Solutions for Tantrums, Rage and Meltdowns.* Shawnee Mission, KS: Autism Asperger, 1999.

Powers, Michael D. *Children with Autism: A Parent's Guide. The Special Needs Collection.* Bethesda, MD: Woodbine House, 2000.

ABOUT THE AUTHOR

Cathi Cohen, a Licensed Clinical Social Worker and Certified Group Psychotherapist, is a leading expert in the field of social skills training in children. This book is based on the many years of collected data and experience of Stepping Stones, a social skills training program for children and their parents, which Cohen created in 1990. Cohen is the founder of In Step, a private group mental health therapy practice that serves families in the metro-Washington, D.C. area. In addition to writing numerous articles and conducting regular workshops for parents, educators, and mental health professionals, Cohen has appeared on several radio and television programs about social skills training. For more information on the Stepping Stones program, please visit www.insteppc.com on the World Wide Web.

Joe Mirabello is a young artist born in Petersburough, England. He has been studying art for over ten years and is currently a university student studying art. If you would like to contact Joe, email him at blankslatejoe @hotmail.com.